Library of
Davidson College

SUMMA PUBLICATIONS, INC.

Thomas M. Hines
Publisher

Norris J. Lacy
Editor-in-Chief

Editorial Board

Benjamin F. Bart
University of Pittsburgh

William Berg
University of Wisconsin

Germaine Brée
Wake Forest University

Michael Cartwright
McGill University

Hugh M. Davidson
University of Virginia

John D. Erickson
Louisiana State University

Wallace Fowlie
Duke University (Retired)

James Hamilton
University of Cincinnati

Freeman G. Henry
University of South Carolina

Edouard Morot-Sir
*University of North Carolina
Chapel Hill*

Jerry C. Nash
University of New Orleans

Albert Sonnenfeld
Princeton University

Ronald W. Tobin
*University of California
Santa Barbara*

Philip A. Wadsworth
University of South Carolina (Retired)

ORDERS:
Box 20725
Birmingham, AL 35216

EDITORIAL ADDRESS:
1904 Countryside
Lawrence, KS 66044

FROM POETRY TO PROSE IN OLD PROVENÇAL

FROM POETRY TO PROSE IN OLD PROVENÇAL

The Emergence of the
Vidas, the *Razos*, and the *Razos de trobar*

Elizabeth Wilson Poe

SUMMA PUBLICATIONS
Birmingham, Alabama
1984

Copyright 1984
Elizabeth Wilson Poe

ISBN 0-917786-33-5
Library of Congress Catalog Number 83-50518

Printed in the United States of America

Contents

I. The Cracks in the Poetic Universe of the *Canso*................... 1

II. *Vidas*: The Prose of the Poetic Life............................. 17

III. *Razos*: The Prose of the Poetic Experience...................... 35

IV. *Las Razos de trobar*: The Prose of Troubadour Poetics.......... 67

V. The Poetics of Copying: The Scribe as Artist
   in the *Chansonniers* and Dante's *Vita Nuova* 83

Notes..97

List of Works Cited... 115

I. The Cracks in the Poetic Universe
of the *Canso*

It was inevitable that the twelfth-century *canso* break down.[1] As a rather narrowly defined genre that, paradoxically, required innovation of every piece within its ranks, it could hardly remain intact against its own internal demands, not to mention the external pressures placed upon it by such historical and social disasters as the Albigensian Crusade and, in literature, the increased emphasis placed on prose around the turn of the thirteenth century. By the late twelfth century the *canso* had established itself within very tight boundaries: A lyric piece in *Lemosi* accompanied by a melody composed especially for it, it consisted typically of five or six *coblas* "stanzas" having eight or nine verses apiece and seven or eight syllables per verse; its subject matter, *fin' amors*, was invariable.[2] And yet, the exigencies of the *canso* structure were equalled and, in a sense, counteracted by the troubadours' inventiveness.

Indeed the troubadours, as they invented, experimented with the *canso* in sophisticated and highly self-conscious ways, and, whenever they stepped beyond the limits of the genre, they were aware of their departure from its domain.[3] Bernart de Ventadorn, for example, recognizes that when he executes a song that has been inspired by some force besides love, though all the rest of the requirements of the *canso* be met, the resulting composition is not rightly called a *canso* but is more aptly designated by the broader term *vers*:

> Car eu non am me ni autrui,
> e fatz esfortz, car sai faire
> bo vers, pois no sui amairé.[4]

Bertran de Born introduces one of his lyric poems with the words: "Mei Sirventés volh far dels reis amdos," thus revealing his awareness of the fact that he is working within a genre other than the *canso*.[5] His ten-syllable verse carries him beyond the customary eight syllables of the *canso*, but, more significantly, his declared subject-matter, a political one, represents a deviation from the *fin' amors* of the *canso* paradigm and makes of his song a *sirventes*.[6]

A similar sensitivity to the limits of the *canso* leads Raimbaut de Vaqueiras to call *Eras quan vey verdeyar* a *descort*[7] because, although the song follows the *canso*-model in the number and length of its *coblas*, the number of syllables per verse, and the nature of its subject-matter, it differentiates itself from the *canso* in its use of languages other than *Lemosi*. After a first stanza in *Lemosi* it continues with stanzas in Genoese, Old French, Gascon, and Galician, respectively. The remarkable multi-lingual *descort* concludes with a ten-verse *tornada* made up of two verses in each of the five dialects used in structuring the song.[8]

Another troubadour, Raimbaut d'Aurenga, begins a certain lyric composition with the following provocative statement:

> Es cotatz, mas no say que s'es
> senhor, so que vuelh comensar.[9]

This opening, though not typical of the *canso*, does seem to fit the pattern of another specific lyric genre, the *gab*.[10] Nevertheless, Raimbaut d'Aurenga refrains from bestowing any ready-made generic label on this particular piece because the last line of every stanza is not in verse at all, but in prose. Hence, none of the conventional lyric classifications applies, and the poet facetiously expresses his recognition of this nonconformity by baptising his song "no·say·que·s'es."[11]

Such permutations of the *canso*—the *vers*, the *sirventes*, the *descort*, the *no-say-que-s'es*, to name only a few—illustrate the range of experimentation possible within the lyric mode. All of these generic permutations, inasmuch as they are themselves lyric, share the fundamental characteristic of incorporating words and music into coherent entities.

The consciousness of the interplay of *motz e sons* is ever present, often explicitly so, throughout the troubadour lyric tradition.[12] Peire Vidal, for example, boasts:

> Ajostar e lassar
> sai tan gent motz e so.[13]

Likewise, Arnaut Daniel declares:

> En cest sonet coind'e leri
> fauc motz e capuig e doli [14]

Though the consolidation of words and music is absolutely essential to the *canso*, even that partnership may be dissolved in some of the more radical departures from the genre. The specific permutations to be discussed in this study—the *vidas, razos,* and Old Provençal manuals of poetic composition—are precisely those which begin by undoing this most fundamental lyric bond. Basing themselves exclusively on the *canso*'s verbality, these three genres operate by extracting words from their original musical context and reassembling them into unsung, unmetered prose.[15] Interestingly, if, on the one hand, the *canso* and its strictly lyric permutations demonstrate a consciousness of the inseparability of words and music, the prose permutations of the *canso*, on the other, reflect a sense that the two components can in fact be separated. The author of the *vida* for Jaufré Rudel, for instance, evaluates Jaufré's work as follows: "Fetz de lieis mains bons vers et ab bons sons, ab paubres motz."[16] While still taking melodies as well as words to be integral parts of the troubadours' compositions, the biographer is nonetheless able to disentangle the two sufficiently to make differential judgments on them, calling the melodies "good" and the words "poor." The composer of the *vida* for Guiraut de Bornelh praises this troubadour for "los sieus maestrals ditz de las soas chansos," thus singling out the poet's words ("ditz") but making no mention of the tunes which must have accompanied them.[17] The biographer for Guiraut de Calanso calls this poet's *cansos* "maestradas" but says of his "ditz" that they were "mal abellivols" (unpopular).[18]

The shift in attitude whereby music came to be of less importance in vernacular lyric poetry is perhaps most strikingly exemplified by comparing the opinion of the poet Jaufré Rudel to that expressed by one of the biographers. Jaufré proclaims unequivocally: "No sap chantar qui so non di."[19] A very different spirit, however, enables the composer of the *vida* for Uc Brunet to say in his account: "e trobet cansos bonas mas non fetz sons."[20]

The self-consciousness which is built into the *canso* goes beyond a feeling for the obvious interplay of *motz* and *sons*. Even in the earliest surviving specimens of troubadour verse we find the poet well aware of his involvement in the poetic process. Frequently the opening verse of the song makes public the troubadour's preoccupation with the creative act in which he is engaged. Guilhem de Peitieu, for example, introduces one song thus:

> Pos de chantar m'es pres talentz,
> farai un vers, don sui dolenz...[21]

Here the experience which motivates the song ("don sui dolenz"), the poetic ego which creates the song ("farai") and the song itself ("vers") are

all intimately and expressly interactive in the verbal articulation under way.
The Comtessa de Dia begins one of her songs as follows:

> A chantar m'er de so q'ieu no volria,
> tant me rancur de lui cui sui amia...[22]

In these verses she brings to the fore the mutual dependency of singing ("chantar"), singer ("ieu"), and experience ("tant me rancur de lui cui sui amia"). Bernart de Ventadorn commences one of his *cansos* with the words:

> Non es meravelha s'eu chan
> melhs de nul autre chantador,
> que plus me tra·l cors vas amor...[23]

In these verses Bernart not only illustrates the close cooperation of the poetic ego ("eu"), the experience ("amor"), and the process of song ("chan"), but also makes an important connection between the quality of the song ("melhs") and the quality of the experience ("plus"). The more he is drawn toward love (the quintessential lyric experience), the better his song will be. The dynamic coequivalence of song, poetic "I", and experience, which the troubadours themselves consciously exploit in verbalizing their *cansos*, may be described schematically as a triangle.[24]

While no *canso* can take shape without simultaneously having recourse to all three points of the so-called lyric triangle, some songs tend more markedly toward one point than toward either of the other two. Hence, one might judge that Jaufré Rudel, for instance, concentrates more deliberately on the experiential angle and that, on the contrary, Arnaut Daniel and other virtuosos of *trobar ric* gravitate more conspicuously toward the angle of craftsmanship.[25]

Just as the *canso* itself plays on the points of the triangle, so also do its prose permutations. Indeed it is partly a function of the relative emphasis placed on one or another of the angles that allows us to classify these prose derivates of the *canso* into distinct genres. Though no one of the prose genres in question is in and of itself representative of any single angle of the triangle, nevertheless, certain correspondences can and should be made. The prose permutation which corresponds most nearly with the poetic ego is the *vida*; that which corresponds most closely with the poetic experience is the *razo*, while that which corresponds best with the verbal craftsmanship of song is the manual for composing troubadour verse, e.g. *Las Razos de trobar*.[26]

Before examining any of these prose offspring of the *canso*, we might do well to look closely at the *canso per se* in order to gain a preliminary understanding of the poetic universe in its wholeness. *Chantars no pot gaire valer,* a song by Bernart de Ventadorn, will serve to represent the genre.[27] Our discussion of the text will focus on three aspects in particular—its treatment of time and space, its organization, and its operation as a self-sufficient literary system, designed not simply to entertain its audience but also to comment critically on itself.

I
    Chantars no pot gaire valer,
    si d'ins dal cor no mou lo chans;
    ni chans no pot dal cor mover,
    si no i es fin' amors coraus.
5   Per so es mos chantars cabaus
    qu'en joi d'amor ai et enten
    la boch' e·ls olhs e·l cor e·l sen.

II
    Ja Deus no·m don aquel poder
    que d'amor no·m prenda talans.
10   Si ja re no·n sabi aver,
    mas chascun jorn m'en vengues maus,
    totz tems n'aurai bo cor sivaus;
    e n'ai mout mais de jauzimen,
    car n'ai bo cor, e m'i aten.

III 15
    Amor blasmen per no-saber,
    fola gens; mas leis no·n es dans,
    c'amors no·n pot ges dechazer,
    si non es amors comunaus.
    Aisso non es amors; aitaus
20   no·n a mas lo nom e·l parven,
    que re non ama si no pren!

IV S'eu en volgues dire lo ver,
  eu sai be de cui mou l'enjans:
  d'aquelas c'amon per aver
25 E son merchadandas venaus!
  Messongers en fos eu e faus!
  Vertat en dic vilanamen;
  e peza me car eu no·n men!

V En agradar et en voler
30 es l'amors de dos fis amans.
  Nula res no i pot pro tener,
  si·lh voluntatz non es egaus.
  E cel es be fols naturaus
  que, de so que vol, la repren
  e·lh lauza so que no·lh es gen.

VI Mout ai be mes mo bon esper,
  cant cela·m mostra bels semblans
  qu'eu plus dezir e volh vezer,
  francha, doussa, fin' e leiaus,
40 en cui lo reis seria saus;
  bel' e conhd', ab cors convinen,
  m'a faih ric ome de nien.

VII Re mais no·n am ni sai temer,
  ni ja res no·m seri' afans,
45 sol midons vengues a plazer,
  c'aicel jorns me sembla nadaus
  c'ab sos bels olhs espiritaus
  m'esgarda; mas so fai tan len
  c'us sols dias me dura cen!

VIII 50 Lo vers es fis e naturaus
  e bos celui qui be l'enten;
  e melher es, qui·l joi aten.

IX
  Bernartz de Ventadorn l'enten,
  e·l di e·l fai, e·l joi n'aten!

The *canso*, like any other piece of organized speech, is linear and must unfold word by word through time; the uniqueness of poetry, however, lies in its capacity to draw attention away from its horizontal development and, thus, in effect, to transcend its own temporality.[28] In *Chantars no pot* Bernart denies time in several ways. In the first place, he weakens the force of conventional divisions into past, present, and future by relying heavily on atemporal modes, e.g. infinitives and subjunctives. The infinitives are: *chantars, valer, mover* in stanza I; *aver* in II; *no saber* and *dechazer* in III; *dire, aver* in IV; *agradar, voler, tener* in V; *vezer* in VI; and *tener, plazer* in VII. The subjunctives include: *don* (8), *prenda* (9), *vengues* (11, 45), *volgues* (22), and *fos* (25). Such verb forms convey virtuality, as opposed to reality. As yet unactivated, they communicate no precise situation in, or specific movement through, time. In the second place, even when the poet activates his verbs by setting them in the indicative mode, he opts, more often than not, to diminish their reality by making them negative. We note, then, a high incidence of *no* (1, 2, 3, 4, 8, 9, 10, 16, 17, 18, 19, 20, 21 twice, 28, 31, 32, 35, 43, 44), which, moreover, on three occasions, is reinforced by the emphatic particle *ja* (8, 10, 44). In the third place Bernart slows the advance of the lyric moment by employing relatively few verbs of action. The majority of verbs in *Chantars no pot* denote being (*esser* 4, 5, 16, 18, 19, 25, 26, 30, 32, 33, 35, 40, 44, 50, 52), emotion (*amar* 21, 24, 43; *dezirar* 38; *voler* 22, 34, 38), state (*poder* 1, 3, 17, 31; *semblar* 46; *aver* 6, 12, 13, 14, 20, 36), mental occupations (*saber* 10, 23, 43; *pesar* 28; *entendre* 6, 51, 53), or various kinds of articulation (*blasmar* 15; *dir* 27, 54; *mentir* 28; *reprendre* 34; *lauzar* 35). In the fourth place, the troubadour obstructs the passage of time by repeating significant words, as, for example: *chantar/chan* (1, 2, 3, 5), *cor/coraus* (2, 3, 4, 7, 12, 14), *amor* (4, 7, 15, 17, 18, 19, 30), *joi* (6, 52, 54), *aten* (14, 52, 54), *mover/mou* (2, 3, 23), *voler/vol* (22, 29, 34, 58), *fin* (4, 30, 39, 50), *enten* (6, 51, 53), and *naturaus* (33, 50). Though we may think that we are going forward, we always seem to end up where we were before; it is as if we were moving in circles, or, perhaps more accurately still, marking time. Finally, the poet seeks to perpetuate the lyric experience by using adverbial expressions on the order of *chascun jorn* (11), *totz tems* (12), *tan len* (48) and verbs like *dura* (49) and *aten* (14, 52, 54), all of which stress duration. By the end of stanza VII ordinary notions of temporality no longer obtain. Christmas is declared at will, and a single day lasts a hundred times as long as it logically should.

Like time, space in *Chantars no pot* is presented in a quintessentially lyric manner. Though there is one explicit geographical reference, i.e. Ventadorn, this name is used more as an epithet modifying "Bernartz" than as a true landmark. The "geography" of the poem is quite simple: "Here" is the domain of the troubadour engaged in song; "there" is the realm of everything and everyone external to him. Bernart's use of demonstratives points up the binary nature of the lyric universe.[29] *Aquel* (8) refers to a strength that the poet does not possess; *aisso* (19) denotes a false love that stands at the opposite pole from Bernart's true one; *aquelas* (24) designates those women whom our poet rejects because they love for money; and *cel* (33) describes the suitor who, unlike Bernart, seeks to manipulate love and does not allow it to enter and rule him. *Cela* (37) is the beloved lady, object of the poet's desire, and in this case the distance established by the demonstrative is partially offset by the juxtaposition of *cela* and *me* as *cela·m*, a grammatical form that fuses into a single unit poet and lady. *Aicel* (46) singles out that day when the troubadour's dream will be fulfilled. An imaginative vision whose existence is purely virtual, *aicel jorns* is removed not so much *in* space as *from* it. As with *cela,* the remoteness of *aicel* is reduced by its proximity to *me*, the creative consciousness who, through the power of words, can actualize the virtual and give it concrete status in the here-and-now locus of the *canso*. The last demonstrative, *celui* (51), refers to the audience, and while our immediate reaction may be a mild resentment that the poet excludes us his listeners from the song by making us third-person outsiders, we are somewhat soothed to see that in the next two verses the troubadour represents himself too as a third-person figure. This process, whereby the poet objectifies both his audience and himself into third-person entities, will be further clarified in the light of our second concern: the tripartite organization of the poem.

Our discussion of the song's structure might well begin with the same observation which launched the foregoing remarks about its treatment of time and space: that is, that as a piece of organized speech which moves along word by word, the *canso* demonstrates undeniable linearity. Thus far we have seen how the poem undercuts temporality, but there is an equally important way in which the *canso* affirms its linear development in time. The troubadour admits that he is singing, that his singing has some duration, and that when he ceases to sing there remains a song which did not exist before, but which has come into being as a result of his activity. With respect to the gradual embodiment of the poem, one can discern three distinct phases: a beginning, or *exordium*; a middle—call it the "body" of the song—and an end, which shall be designated by its Provençal name, *tornada*.

The *exordium* consists of the first stanza: In it the poet sets the wheels in motion for the creative operation which engages him. The stanza is divided into two parts; vv. 1-4 constitute an impersonal gnomic formula about the inspiration for song, while vv. 5-7 present the application of the general statement to the poet's personal experience.[30] The *exordium* traces movement from the outside in: External truth filters into the poet's creative self, and, at another level, the audible verses filter into the recreative self of the audience. Poet and listener alike are drawn into song. The composition moves irreversibly forward as we are caught up inside it. The evolution from the virtual *chantars* "singing" (1) to the actual *chans* "song" (4) adumbrates the growth of the *canso* as a whole. It is noteworthy that Bernart will not mention *chantar* or *chan* again after the *exordium*. This is because of the change in perspective wrought by these opening verses. Having been led out of the external world, we are one with the poet inside the creative act; any further reminder of the growing structure of the song around us would divert our attention from the central event—the emergence of the poetic vision. Thus, the *exordium* plunges us into the poetic consciousness, but, besides that, it introduces all the important thematic and structural elements of the poem.[31] *Amor, joi* and *enten* will serve as key terms throughout the song, and the human organs enumerated in the last verse of the stanza—mouth, eyes, heart, and mind—will provide the units upon which the "body" of the song will be built.

The body of the poem extends from stanzas II through VII. Each of these stanzas emanates directly from the *exordium*. The word *cor* in the final verse of the opening stanza offers the clue for the development of stanza II, *boch*, is the key for stanza IV, and *olhs* for stanza VI; stanzas III and V both seem to develop from *sen*.[32] There is a nice, perhaps deliberate alternation between those stanzas which contain *eu* and those which do not. The precedent for this play of the first and third persons is established in the *exordium*, where, as indicated above, the first four verses are in the third person and the last three are in the first person. Stanza II has an *eu*; stanza III has none; IV has an *eu*; V has none. VI has an *eu*; at this point the symmetry breaks down, for stanza VII, like VI, revolves around *eu*.

But it is not just the unexpected presence of *eu* which makes VII a remarkable stanza. At the risk of being contradicted by as yet undiscovered versions of the text, I would venture to argue that stanza VII has to occur where it does because it marks the culmination of the poetic vision and thus signals the approach to the *canso*'s unavoidable end. It is here that the woman returns the poet's gaze; it is now that time has been conquered, for Christmas is decreed by personal whim rather than liturgical convention, and a single day stretches on for twenty-four hundred hours. The final word of the stanza, *cen*, echoes the *sen* which we have not heard since the close of the *exordium*. Instantly, the vision is over; the spell, broken; and we are, through purely aural association (*sen/cen*), snapped back to the point at which we were about to enter the body of the song.

The third and final part of the poem is composed of two short stanzas, or *tornadas*.[33] Their opening words "lo vers" indicate that the poet has assumed a new stance in relation to the poetic process. He is no longer on the inside of the poem looking out. He has moved away, and, from his new vantage point, can perceive the completed composition as an independent entity, a *vers*. If the first stanza marked the threshold over which we crossed from the outside world into the poem, the *tornadas* constitute the threshold across which we pass from the *canso* back to external reality. The two *tornadas* taken as a block parallel the structure of the *exordium*. In both of these threshold zones of the song, there is a movement from the general to the specific. In the *exordium* the impersonal *chantars* (1) gives way to *mos chantars* (5), while in the *tornadas* the unspecified subject of *enten, celui* (51), cedes to the poet himself, *Bernartz de Ventadorn* (53).

True to their etymology, the *tornadas* return to many of the conspicuous motifs of the song. *Ver, fis, naturaus, enten, joi, aten, di*, and *fai* have all been used earlier. In comparing their final occurrences with their previous ones, we can better assess the movement of the *canso* as a whole. For example, *ver*, first employed in connection with the poet's wish to express himself ("eu...volgues dir lo ver" 22), now stands free and no longer needs the poet for its actualization ("lo vers es..." 50). The attribute *fis* also follows a significant progression: Associated originally with abstract *Amors* "Love" (4), it is next linked to two unspecified lovers, or *amans* (30), then to the particular object of Bernart's desire *cela* (39), and, ultimately, to *vers* (50), the completed song. *Enten*, for its part, refers originally to the poet (6) and, in *tornada* I, to the audience (51); this verb, in the *exordium*, suggests the understanding which the artist pours into his creative activity, whereas the *enten* of the first *tornada* connotes the understanding by means of which the audience perceives and re-creates for itself the finished work. The subject of *aten*, like that of *enten*, switches from the poet to the audience and then, in the second *tornada*, back to the poet. Such shifting of the grammatical subject from poet to audience to poet implies that Bernart considers the creative process a dialogue between himself and his listener. The verb *dir* illustrates a characteristically lyric evolution, from the infinitive "volgues dir" (22) to the present indicative *di* (54). Meanwhile, *fai* also evolves, though differently from *dir*. In the central section of the song, the lady, with whose image the poet is obsessed, acts as the subject of *far* (42, 48). A reversal takes place in the *tornada*, however, when the poet himself becomes the subject of *fai* (54). Through the exercise of his creative faculty, which he regarded earlier as a composite of distinct organs (*boch', olhs, cor, sen*), the troubadour has achieved a unified image of himself as "Bernartz de Ventadorn." In the end, then, it is Bernart, initially portrayed as a helpless victim of Love's power, who reigns triumphant, for he alone has the authority which comes from making songs.

The function of the *tornadas* is to effect closure, and so they do. They call to mind one last time the central motifs of the *canso* and bring us back to where we began—in joy. Moreover, the poet, by referring to himself in the final verses of his composition by name and in the third person, conflates the first and third persons, which have been in tension throughout the song. That tension now resolved, the poem can come to rest. . .

Or can it? There remains an implicit ambiguity in the set-up, for the poet who can look upon himself in the third person is not totally contained in that third-person figure. There is a necessary poetic *eu* who utters the name "Bernartz" and who stays locked inside the structure of the song even when the historical Bernart de Ventadorn detaches himself from his creation. A second ambiguity in the poem's ending resides in its last word, *aten*.[34] The verb *aten* indicates an activity that continues over a length of time. If we press this reflection a bit further, we note that *aten* suggests not only duration but also direction; it looks by definition to the future. Even in the present indicative it implies an event which has yet to occur. Thus, *aten* as the ultimate word, instead of bringing the song to rest, keeps it hanging in perpetual suspension.

To summarize: Our examination of the parts of the poem has made it clear that the song does advance. From the first immobile *chantars* to the last dynamic *aten* we have come a long way. And yet, the *canso*'s persistent desire to be free of the constraints of time and space is at least partially realized in the end with the unsettling paradoxes of a third-person "I" and an open-ended close.

Our third concern with respect to this *canso* is to show how it contains all the elements necessary for the making of a *vida,* a *razo* or a manual on *trobar.* This discussion may seem a bit contrived, since there are in fact no *vidas, razos* or manuals on composition based upon this particular song. Nevertheless, there is in *Chantars no pot,* as in practically any piece of this genre, the potential for development along one or more of these three generic lines.

In the way of biographical data, the *canso* informs us of the poet's name and provenance: He is "Bernartz" from "Ventadorn." In addition, v. 42 tells us that the troubadour was transformed by his lady from *nien* "nothing" into a *ric ome* "man of prestige." While *ric* for the poet undoubtedly connotes power and spiritual wealth, the word leaves itself open to interpretation as wealthy in a material sense too.[35] Consequently, it is not hard to imagine that the composer of a *vida* might have taken this verse as indicative of a literal rise through the economic strata of society. Indeed it happens that the actual *vida* for Bernart, though its source of information is probably something other than *Chantars no pot,* recounts just such a success story.[36] Bernart is portrayed as a poor-boy-makes-good whose father was a humble oven stoker at the Castle of Ventadorn. The gifted son learned the art of inventing songs, acquired courtly manners, and eventually won favor from both the Viscount of Ventadorn and his wife, the viscountess.

Moreover, still staying within the bounds of this *canso*, one can find all the threads required for the weaving of a *razo.* The lyric text names protagonists in "Bernartz" and *cela* and antagonists in the *fola gen* and *aquelas c'amon per aver.* It provides a theme, *amor,* and a counter-theme, *enjans.* It affords a concrete setting with "Ventadorn." It even suggests a plot, for the striking image of stanza VII can be pulled apart and reworked into an extravagant narrative. Imagine the following non-existent but perfectly plausible "*razo.*" The poet, convinced by his adversaries that his lady, "X," had been unfaithful to him, refused for some time to seek her company. One Christmas Day he recognized the error of his harsh judgment of her and presented himself at her court to ask forgiveness. Lady "X," upon learning that the poet was there, was secretly pleased but decided to punish him first for his infidelity. She sent word for him to wait until she should receive him later that day. The contrite poet remained, obedient, a full hundred days before she admitted him into her sight. And that is why he invented the *canso* which says:

> c'aicel jorns me sembla nadaus
> c'ab sos bels olhs espiritaus
> m'esgarda; mas so fai tan len
> c'us sols dias me dura cen!

Finally, the ideas expressed in this *canso* could conceivably furnish the basis for a manual on the art of composition. Bernart de Ventadorn begins *Chantars no pot* by explaining the prerequisites for a worthy *canso:* The song must originate from deep within the heart, and only when that heart is completely consumed by love. Viewing himself in light of this evaluation of the poetic craft, Bernart declares that his own singing is excellent because his mouth, eyes, heart, and mind are all in the power of love's joy. Oddly enough, however, while both the *exordium* and the *tornadas* reveal the poet in a state of joy, euphoria does not prevail throughout the *canso*. In the fourth stanza we find him prey to a despair which is the very antithesis of the joy which first inspired his song. Bernart sums up this feeling in the last verse of stanza IV with the words "peza me" (28). It seems a bit surprising that the troubadour can have a heavy heart in the central part of the poem, where one would think that his imagination should know no constraints. Here, though, we hit upon the essential paradox: The poet's imagination, operating purely in an imaginary universe of its own creation, is nonetheless bound to the truth of external reality. The tension between truth and imagination reaches a climax right in the middle of the song, where the poet cries: "Messongers en fos eu e faus!" (26). But to lie is an impossible option for the poet because his belief in the seriousness of his craft prevents him from being able to take words lightly. He cannot cover up ugly reality with pretty images, since those images, being deceptive, would themselves be ugly.

By serving the truth with his words, Bernart produces a *ver*—note the play on words between *ver* "truth" and *ver* "verse"—which he can confidently describe as "fis e naturaus" (50).[37] Whatever frustrations the poet may have experienced in composing his *canso*, he concludes on an optimistic note. He announces hopefully that, now that the *canso* has been completed, he awaits joy from it. What kind of reward is he expecting: recognition of his poetic skill, gifts from an approving patron, or love from the mysterious lady celebrated in this piece? No matter. What counts is Bernart's strong belief in the value of his craft.[38]

In making the transition from the *canso* to the *vidas* and *razos*, we might remark, based on our analysis of *Chantars no pot*, that even the most tightly sealed poetic composition has leaks. Indeed, cracks in the fundamentally self-referential lyric universe are necessary if anyone other than the poet is to be privy to the truth contained in the poem. The first such crack which I would cite derives from the *canso*'s implicit awareness of a reality external to itself. The song provides various openings, or means of access, whereby one may enter into, and emerge from, its world; in affording openings of this kind, the poem assumes, of course, the existence of a realm besides its own. The *exordium* and *tornada(s)* serve as the logical thresholds between the natural world of the poet and his listeners and the artificial universe of the *canso*. Sometimes, however, an allusion to an historic character, event, or place may intrude right in the very heart of a lyric piece.[39] Moreover, even without having to name specific people, places, or occurrences, the *canso* points beyond itself. Beyond the here and now of *cai* is a necessary *lai*; beyond the poet, *eu*, is the object of his desire, *cela*; and beyond the poet within the poem is the one who lives outside it.

Another crack in the largely atemporal lyric sphere results from the diachrony of the tradition in which the poem participates. The individual *canso* makes sense only because of the poems which have preceded it. It is because of this tradition that associations such as *pretz* with *valor* or *jauzen* with *pensiu* can be understood immediately and without explanation.[40] Likewise, it is soley on the basis of a rich poetic heritage that *joi* can be equated with *amor*.[41] Thus, the *canso* does not operate in a vacuum;[42] on the contrary, it depends on the past to give it meaning.

An additional crack in the essentially circular lyric sphere comes from the almost inevitable narrative content of the *canso*. Any poem, no matter how short or how lyrical, tends to have a narrative, or potentially narrative, component.[43] Thus, in addition to conforming to its own poetic laws, the *canso* must, to a lesser extent, recognize the prosaic laws governing the flow of events in the everyday world.

Perhaps the most distinctive crack in the private world generated by the *canso* is a product of its transmission. Despite its high degree of self-reflectiveness, the *canso* remained public in that it was performed.[44] Hermeticism for the troubadours was not possible in the same way as it was for, say, Mallarmé.[45] A modern poet can occasion a private, silent confrontation between himself and his reader through letters on a printed page. But the troubadours worked within a tradition that was largely oral. The *cansos* which they composed were destined to be sung by a *jongleur* before a number of people. There was, then, an unavoidable tension between the private realm created by the song and the public setting in which it had to be verbalized. One way in which the troubadours reduced this tension was to use *senhals*, or pseudonyms.[46] In giving secret names to the *personae* of the *canso*, the poet discouraged connections between the men and women mentioned in his song and those assembled in the audience. Nevertheless, the fact that the troubadours felt compelled to invent *senhals* in the first place attests to the natural tendency for contemporary listeners to interpret these poems as referring to real, rather than imaginary, men and women.

Just how long the troubadour lyric universe survived before such cracks made it begin to disintegrate is problematic. Certain *cansos* may have been introduced by *vidas* or *razos* at their initial performances. Other songs may have existed for a century or more without any formal explanation in prose of whom or what they were about. Still others probably continued indefinitely to be sung without a prefatory *vida* or *razo*. All that is certain concerning the origins of the *vidas* and *razos* is that by the thirteenth century there was a substantial body of them deemed worthy of inclusion in certain of the *chansonniers* being compiled at that time.

The *vidas* and *razos*, as they have come down to us through the *chansonniers*, number approximately 225 and portray 101 troubadours.[47] *Vidas* are biographical statements usually only four or five lines long and rarely exceeding fifteen or twenty; *razos* are little stories which claim to recount how a particular poem came to be. The majority of *vidas* and *razos* are anonymous, most likely the work of *jongleurs* who performed troubadour songs.[48] There are only two named authors, Uc de Saint Circ and Miquel de la Tor, and exactly how many (if any) biographies they may have composed cannot be determined.[49] The original purpose of *vidas* and *razos* was to introduce poems, but, with time, they came to be regarded as entities in their own right. By the fourteenth century compilers of several *chansonniers* saw fit to group *vidas* and *razos* together, apart from the poems which had given rise to them.[50]

Vidas and *razos*, though often of dubious historicity and limited critical value, nevertheless, enhance our understanding of the troubadour lyric tradition in particular and of the nature of poetry and prose in general.[51] Even in the instances where a *vida* or *razo* describes the same event as a certain poem, the biographical point of view differs radically from the lyric one. At the very least, two changes take place in the transposition of a given incident from a lyric poem to a *vida* or *razo*: The poetic "I" becomes a third-person figure, and the present tense of lyric poetry gives way to a set of past tenses in prose.[52] Now, the *vida* as a relatively unself-conscious genre restricts itself to this third-person past; the preterite is the tense which it characteristically employs, though the imperfect occurs with some frequency as well. Both of these tenses define themselves with respect to the moment of the event, rather than the moment of discourse.[53] Specifically, then, the *vidas* situate themselves in a past whose unique frame of reference is the troubadour lyric tradition. The *razos* work like the *vidas*, except that as a more sophisticated, more self-conscious genre, they permit an "I," the narrator of the story in progress; moreover, the introduction of this narrative "I" prompts a new tense, i.e. the *passé composé*, which, in distinction to the preterite and the imperfect, is defined with respect to the moment of discourse.[54] Hence, the *razos* have a double frame of reference: Their central narrative core, like that of the *vidas*, is oriented around the lyric tradition, while their outer frame comprehends whichever other *razos* may be part of the present moment of discourse.

Thus, the *vidas and razos* project a very different world from that of the *cansos*. Focusing on third-person figures, they refer primarily to a reality outside themselves. Set in the past, they look beyond the self-centeredness of the present moment. Space in the *vidas* and *razos* is linear, not binary as in the *cansos*; its organizing principle is contiguity. Each castle, town, church, etc. borders on another. Space in these prose genres, and especially in the *vidas*, tends to be named and classified, and a single locus, Ventadorn for example, may participate simultaneously in several overlapping referential schemes—feudal, ecclesiastical, historical, cultural.[55]

The extroverted world of the *vidas* and *razos* is peculiar, in that its people, events, and places are precisely those of the self-referential lyric world. In a sense, then, what is represented in the *vidas* and *razos* is the introverted lyric world turned inside out.

II. *Vidas*: the Prose of the Poetic Life

Vida names those little prose narratives which attempt to formulate in the span of a few sentences the essence of a troubadour's whole life. Their facts may come from poems, historical documents, or the imagination of their creators. Because in the Middle Ages the boundaries between such categories were fluid, the *vida* could, and characteristically did, draw from a combination of sources.[1] Moreover, the integration of "historical" and poetic fact within the individual account was not merely an artistic possibility, but also and even more fundamentally, a generic necessity, inasmuch as the primary purpose of the *vida* was to provide a vital link between the world in which the poet lived and the world which he created.

It is worth stressing that the *vida* served as "a" and not as "the" vital link between a particular set of poems and the aristocratic culture in which they were performed, for if ideally there can be only one *vida* per poet, in fact there are sometimes several.[2] Different biographers selecting different elements from the various sources at hand could effectively construct disparate lives for a single troubadour. For example, Marcabru is portrayed in one *vida* as an abandoned child and in another as the acknowledged son of a lady called Na Bruna.[3] Such radical discrepancies are, however, rare. More frequently we find that the differences among multiple *vidas* are slight. MS *R*'s account of, say, Guillem de Balaun is generally more concise than MS *H*'s.[4] And the *I-K* rendition of Jaufré Rudel's life is more compact than the *A-B* version.[5] Changes in the *vidas* could have been wrought by either *jongleurs* or clerks. But in either case such modifications need not disturb us because we can assume that what medieval audiences expected from the *vidas* was the flavor, more than the facts, of the lives of individual troubadours. Let us look, then, at how the *vidas* treat three of the best-known exemplars of the Old Provençal lyric tradition—namely, Guiraut de Borneill, Arnaut Daniel, and Jaufré Rudel.

It is appropriate to place Guiraut de Borneill first in our discussion because the thirteenth-century clerks seemed to agree that that was where he belonged. His *vida* and poems occur at or near the beginning of all four of the thirteenth-century *chansonniers* which preserve them.[6] The particular version of the text cited here is that of MS *K*, as it has been transcribed and edited by J. Boutière and I.-H. Schutz.[7] Here, as elsewhere in this study, the Boutière-Schutz edition of the biographies of the troubadours will be taken as authoritative.

Guiraut de Borneill
Vida

Girautz de Borneill si fo de Limozi, de l'encontrada d'Esiduoill, d'un ric castel del viscomte de Lemoges. E fo hom de bas afar, mas savis hom fo de letras e de sen natural. E fo meiller trobaire que negus d'aquels qu'eron estat denan ni foron apres lui; per que fo apellatz maestre dels trobadors, et es ancar per toz aquels que ben entendon subtils ditz ni ben pauzatz d'amor ni de sen. Fort fo honratz per los valenz homes e per los entendenz e per las dompnas qu'entendian los sieus maestrals ditz de las soas chansos.

E la soa vida si era aitals que tot l'invern estava en escola et aprendia letras, e tota la estat anava per cortz e menava ab se dos cantadors que cantavon las soas chansos. Non volc mais muiller, e tot so qu'el gazaingnava dava a sos paubres parenz et a la eglesia de la villa on el nasquet, la quals glesia avia nom, et a ancaras, Saint Gervas.

Et aici son escritas gran ren de las soas chansos.

The opening formula "Girautz de Borneill si fo de Limozi" sets the scene. It situates us in space with "Borneill" and "Limozi" and in time with the past tense *fo*. This phrase summons forth a poetic tradition by naming the troubadour, Guiraut de Borneill, at the same time that it integrates itself into a prose genre—the *vida*—by conforming to the characteristic exordial pattern of "poet's name *si fo de*+place name." If the primary function of a *vida* is to establish a temporal and spatial frame for a body of lyric poems, then there is a sense in which we may take the first seven words as the crux of the biography and regard all that follows as an amplification of this initial statement.

The setting "Limozi" connotes both linguistically and geographically the entire troubadour lyric universe. The *vida* does not leave this world intact, however, but proceeds immediately to break it down into smaller units—first the region of Esiduoill and then the castle of the Viscount of Limoges. This compartmentalization of space suggests a world perceived as a network of separate, named loci. The lyric universe, though recalled by "Limozi," is no longer wholly operative, but has fragmented.

The first verb *si fo* places us in the simple past, but time in the biography of Guiraut is by no means simple. Indeed there are two separate past tenses used: the preterite and the imperfect, with consistent discriminations made between them.[8] As in modern French, the medieval preterite may signify a discrete action completed in the past. It is with this intent that the biographer selects the preterite to report that Guiraut *nasquet* "was born." More frequently, though, the preterites in this text conform to a usage which no longer obtains, that is, to denote permanent states or conditions which constitute the very essence of an object. We learn, for example, that Guiraut "was" from Limousin, he "was" of low estate, he "was" knowledgeable, he "was" the best troubadour, he "was" called the master of the troubadours, and he "was" honored by everyone who heard him, all of the above being communicated to us by the preterite *fo*.

Meanwhile the other past tense, the imperfect, generally served to indicate repeated or habitual activity, and it is in this sense that the composer of the *vida* chooses it for the verbs of action: *aprendia, menava, cantavon, gazaingnava, dava*. Another function of the imperfect was descriptive, but whereas the preterite could be used to describe the essence of a thing, the imperfect was employed to describe its accidents. A subtle distinction for us perhaps, but Guiraut's biographer seems to observe it, for after the monotony of six *fo*'s he startles us by selecting the imperfect of the verb *esser* in the sentence which begins: "E la soa vida si era. . ." *Era* is logical here in that what the author proceeds to explain about the poet's life is not its intrinsic nature but the external occupations which came to be associated with it.

Two verb forms in this *vida* might at first seem unusual; these are the preterite *volc* in the terse statement "Non volc mais muiller" and the imperfect *avia* in the clause "la quals glesia avia nom." The choice of *volc* emphasizes the finality of the troubadour's desire to remain celibate, a resolution which was apparently as fundamental to his character as the fact that he was *savis* and *honratz*. The selection of the imperfect *avia* over the preterite *ac* distinguishes the extended state of "having" from the one-time act of "acquiring." Thus, one finds reflected in this rather typical *vida* an appreciation of these two past tenses which is not merely consistent, but indeed quite refined.

Nor is time in the *vida* for Guiraut de Borneill restricted to the past. Guiraut is made to participate in two different temporal schemes: his own lifetime and posterity. By virtue of the name which he earned for himself, he transcended the limits of his natural life and came to be regarded, at least by his biographer, as the best troubadour of all times. The *vida* proclaims Guiraut as the master troubadour, a distinction which, we are told, he still holds. Through the juxtaposition of the preterite *fo* and the present *es*, the composer of the *vida* stresses Guiraut de Borneill's status not only in a bygone, but also in an ongoing, literary tradition.

Having examined the spatial and temporal frame within which this *vida* unfolds, we look now more closely at its organization. The first paragraph situates Guiraut geographically, socially, intellectually, and professionally. The second paragraph describes how in winter Guiraut remained in school as a teacher and how in summer he traveled from court to court in the company of two singers who had the job of performing his songs before the public. Beyond this, the account has little else to report, for Guiraut was interested neither in finding a wife nor in amassing a fortune, preferring to contribute whatever money he earned to his parents and to the church of his native town.

By the end of the *vida* the world generated by the *exordium* has been turned upside down. The account, which began in a castle, ends in a church. Having started in the past, it concludes in the present. The one constant is that Guiraut de Borneill remains at the center of things. To call the centrality of Guiraut a constant does not necessarily imply that his image is static. Once firmly established in the text as the master troubadour, Guiraut is made to conform to the ideal of the clerk, too. He leads a double existence, as poet and scholar. His scholarship, willful celibacy, and self-imposed poverty suggest a clerkly life. In this way the *vida* for Guiraut de Borneill celebrates troubadour and clerk alike. The biographer, though he never names himself and never overtly imposes a first-person viewpoint on his narrative, may perhaps have been a clerk who unobtrusively bestowed glory on his own manner of life by having the greatest of the troubadours imitate him. The blatant disparity between the initial and final images of Guiraut gives a clue to the general organization of the text. In living like a clerk, Guiraut was no less a troubadour. Every trait attributed to him in the *vida* applied throughout his life. He incorporated all these things simultaneously. We begin to understand that, despite the biographer's skillful manipulation of verb tenses, chronology does not explain the arrangement of events. This *vida* does not move forward through time, but, rather, like a pendulum, swings back and forth between extremes—summer and winter, school and court, castle and church. It is this kind of tension which provides the basic structure of the account.

This text arouses interest not only by what it says, but by what it chooses not to say. It seems odd, for example, that Guiraut, whom the *vida* for Peire d'Auvergne designated quite clearly as the inventor of the *canso*, should not be cited for this notable achievement in his own biography.[9] It is possible, perhaps even probable, that the composer of the *vida* for Guiraut was not the same as had made the *vida* for Peire and, consequently, may either not have known or not have believed that this troubadour created the *canso*-form. A second omission relates to the first: Although the biographer does indeed recognize Guiraut's poems as being *cansos*, he tells us nothing about them except that they had "maestrals ditz." He makes no comment as to whether they were many or few, good or bad, complex or plain, laudatory or disapproving. The author's silence on this point is an effective device, to be sure, for by not saying anything specific about the style of Guiraut's verse, he leaves us free to imagine whatever we like. He simply disposes us favorably toward the troubadour without seeking to dictate what we should look for in his poems.[10] Such vagueness works particularly well for a corpus of *cansos* as vast and varied as Guiraut de Borneill's. *Chansonniers I* and *K*, for instance, preserve 48 texts which, all told, display a remarkable diversity in style and tone.[11]

The attribution of clerkly characteristics to a troubadour, as in the account for Guiraut, is by no means a generalized feature of the *vida* as a genre. In fact, our next text, the *vida* for Arnaut Daniel, is slanted in the opposite direction, toward the *jongleur* instead of the clerk.[12] Indeed Arnaut started out as a man of letters but quickly abandoned scholarly endeavors to become a *jongleur*.

Arnaut Daniel
Vida

Arnautz Daniel si fo d'aquella encontrada don fo N'Arnautz de Meruoill, de l'evesquat de Peiregors, d'un castel que a nom Ribairac, e fo gentils hom. Et amparet ben letras e delectet se en trobar. Et abandonet las letras, et fetz se joglars, e pres una maniera de trobar en caras rimas, per que soas cansons no son leus ad entendre ni ad aprendre. Et amet una auta domna de Gascoingna, muiller d'En Guillem de Buovilla, mas non fo cregut que la domna li fezes plaiser en dreit d'amor; per qu'el dis:

[29, 10] Eu son Arnautz qu'amas l'aura
E chatz la lebre ab lo bou
E nadi contra suberna. . .

As in the previous text, the opening sentence of the *vida* for Arnaut surrounds the poet by a comprehensive poetic realm which immediately narrows, first to the bishopric of Périgord and then to the castle of Ribérac. On the whole, time in Arnaut's *vida* is straightforward. This *vida* begins in typical fashion with the intransitive *fo*, but switches right away to transitive verbs—*amparet, delectet, abandonet, fetz, pres, amet, dis*—the poet being the active subject in each case. Although inflected verbs are the only grammatical forms which can bring an action to pass, other parts of speech may suggest a dynamic process at work. For instance, the substantivized infinitives—*trobar, entendre, aprendre*—do not refer to a solid object called "song" but to the process whereby the song is composed, understood, and retained. The preterites in Arnaut's *vida* convey a series of irreversible actions which must take us somewhere. The obvious question, of course, is: Where? The clearest way of assessing our displacement is to contrast our situation in the opening words of the account with where we find ourselves in the end. In a way, it seems that we have made a full circle because the text both opens and closes with the identification of the poet. Yet we soon recognize that, despite such apparent circularity, the movement of the story is essentialy linear. The "Arnaut" of the *exordium* is a third-person character who lived in a remote time and place, while the final "Arnaut" defines a first-person poet who, through his song, lives in the present. Thus, we have progressed. From our original stance as spectators looking back at a historical personage far-removed from us, we have penetrated into the ever-present voice of a lyric "I."

Having determined that our ultimate destination is to become integrated into the poetic process, we examine the means by which the composer of the *vida* directs us towards this goal. A chronological sequence of preterites, while it does afford some advancement through time, cannot by itself bring us up to the present. Therefore, the author of this account makes occasional use of the present tense in order to abolish momentarily the distance separating us, the *vida*, and Arnaut's songs. The present first occurs in the expression *a nom*, associated with a place name—the castle

Ribérac. An important aspect of geography lies in its capacity to fuse past and present, for the metonymic relationship between a dead poet and an extant landmark confers a kind of immortality on the poet. That the particular predicate used here should be *aver nom* warrants remarking, for, as we shall soon discover, the entire *vida* is built around a play of names and naming. The second example of the present tense is the third-person plural of the verb *esser* in the clause: "cansons son. . ." *Canso* activated by a present-tense verb serves its customary function of designating the creation which outlives its creator and, more specifically, prepares us for the end of the *vida* where, through words taken from *En cest sonet*, the poet Arnaut will make himself present.[13]

Neither of these two insertions of the present tense need surprise us, since we have seen precedent for both in the *vida* for Guiraut de Borneill. Arnaut's castle, which "a nom," is analogous to Guiraut's church, which was and still is called Saint-Gervais. Moreover, the words "cansons son" in this text recall the same words from the other account. The third occurrence of the present tense in this *vida* differs significantly, however, from the other two. Arnaut, speaking for himself through his song, announces: "I am . . . I gather. . .I chase. . .I swim. . ." We realize now that the entire narrative has been moving toward these final, enigmatic assertions. The present tense of these last four verbs is neither that of the impersonal, historical landmark Ribérac nor that of the finished songs which survive their author; it is, rather, the present of the nascent lyric creation, which is re-enacted with each new confrontation of text and audience.

Yet, in addition to the interjection of present-tense verbs, the composer of the *vida* steers us toward our goal through other devices as well. As is often the case, the *exordium* foreshadows the further development of the narrative. The formula which begins the *vida* for Arnaut Daniel deviates slightly from the conventional pattern of "troubadour's name *si fo de* + place name" in that, instead of naming the *encontrada* outright, the biographer identifies it periphrastically as "that area whence came Arnaut de Marouill." The ingenious substitution of the anticipated toponym by a reference to Arnaut de Marouill places us securely in a poetic universe and relates Arnaut Daniel to one of the other great poets of the tradition. Furthermore, the mention of the particular troubadour Arnaut de Marouill sets up a clever play of *adnominatio* on the name "Arnaut." "Arnaut" occurs three times in the *vida*—first to introduce our poet, then to distinguish him from the other Arnaut, and finally to permit him to identify himself. The naming of the troubadour, as executed first in the narrative proper and then in the excerpt from the *canso*, points up an intrinsic difference between *vida* and *canso*. In the prose account the poet is defined by an outsider who takes care to avoid possible misunderstanding. The conscientious biographer gives us Arnaut's family name, "Daniel," and differentiates him from the other famous troubadour bearing the same Christian name. There can, then, be no confusion in the prose rendering as to who is meant. In the extract from the *canso*, on the other hand, there is much more room for ambiguity, as the poet reports simply: "I am Arnaut." Both the biographer and the poet proceed to fill us in a little on what this Arnaut is like. In prose the description of Arnaut follows a logical order. We learn of his origin, training, style of poetry, and love for a particular Gascon lady. The verses, for their part, present a very different picture. Here the poet describes himself as the one who gathers up the breeze, chases after the rabbit while riding on an ox, and swims against the current. A man who attempts the impossible, the Arnaut of the song finds himself constantly at odds with nature.

Now, the disparity between the prosaic and poetic portrayals of the poet brings us to consider to what extent, if at all, the biographer has prepared us for the three verses with which he concludes. It seems to me that the sentence in this *vida* which sets the scene for the closing *tornada* is: "Las soas cansons no son leus ad entendre ni ad aprendre." This terse commentary pertains to Arnaut's songs in three ways. In the first place, the remark that his *cansos* are "no leus," in conjunction with an earlier reference to *caras rimas*, establishes Arnaut as a poet of the *trobar ric*, or ornate style.[14] In the second place, in saying that the songs are "no leus," the biographer flatters us, the audience; for his admission that Arnaut Daniel's songs are hard to understand consoles us in the event that we comprehend nothing of the poems and praises us in the event that we manage to discern something of their meaning. Finally, the judgment that the songs "no son leus ad aprendre," that is, that they are difficult to memorize, glorifies that performer who can quote from them as readily as the author of this *vida* is doing for us here.[15]

But we still have not determined how the general commentary provided by this *vida* elucidates the meaning of the specific verses cited. If we apply what we have been told in the *vida* to these verses, we discover that Arnaut's depiction of himself as fighting against nature invites two different but compatible interpretations. First, the biographer has reported that the troubadour's attentions to his lady from Gascony were most likely never repaid. Thus, the image of Arnaut battling against great odds may be understood, at least in part, as an allusion to his frustration as a lover.[16] Second, having learned that Arnaut Daniel composed *caras rimas* and deliberately produced songs of great difficulty, we may view his struggle against the natural, the logical order of things as the process whereby he creates his song. Like all poets, Arnaut works within artificial constraints, effectively turning the world upside down in his quest for poetic over rational truth. Consequently, the most fundamental obstacles for him are neither the natural forces of wind and stream, nor even the emotional turmoil of an impossible love, but rather the rigid patterns which he has established for the song in progress.[17]

Our examination of how the prose portion of the *vida* prepares for the three verses which conclude it brings us to reflect on how these verses prepare for a whole group of poems by Arnaut Daniel. The verses cited at the end of the *vida* constitute the *tornada* of *En cest sonet coind'e leri*, the first song recorded under the rubric "Arnaut Daniel" in *Chansonnier I*. Thus, the transition from *vida* to poems, at least according to the arrangement of *I*, is smooth since we are already inside the particular lyric "I" of *En cest sonet* when the *canso* actually begins. The *vida*'s reference to Arnaut's unrequited love lays the foundation for *En cest sonet*, whose theme is the unattainable woman.[18] The *vida* states, and the *canso* confirms, that this lady provides the inspiration for Arnaut's song: "mon chantar, que de liei mou." Furthermore, the *vida*'s brief commentary on Arnaut's technique serves as an appropriate preparation for *En cest sonet* to the extent that this *canso* is itself a commentary on poetic technique. The troubadour sings of planing, finishing, and filing his words until they fit together perfectly.[19]

To summarize, we note that this *vida* revolves entirely around Arnaut's career as troubadour and *jongleur*. We are told nothing about who his parents were, nor are we given the precise name of the *encontrada* where he was born. He is presented uniquely in the light of a poetic tradition, his chosen heritage. Within the domain of versemaking the troubadour boldly makes his own way as he *fetz se* and *pres*, finally succeeding in establishing his identity as poet: "eu son Arnautz." Every affirmation in the prose moves us nearer to our ultimate resting place inside the poem. Even the mention of

Arnaut's futile love for the lady from Gascony marks a step forward because *cansos* are, without exception, about love, though sometimes, as here, unrequited. The *vida*'s conclusion encourages us to view the whole corpus of Arnaut Daniel's poems in terms of the image of the craftsman in rebellion against the natural order of things. This image both alerts us to the obstacles which the poet sets up for himself and prepares us to appreciate his masterly conquest of them.

The third *vida*, the well-known story of Jaufré Rudel,[20] differs substantially from the two preceding ones, for, rather than concentrate on public information about the poet's social status, career, and reputation, this account deals exclusively with a private love affair. The subtlety and grace with which this biography proceeds tempts us to associate it with a later, more sophisticated narrative art than that normally operative in the *vidas*; however, manuscript evidence attests to the relatively early date of composition of this text, contained as it is in all four of the extant thirteenth-century *vida*-bearing *chansonniers*. Though its well-wrought plot may make this account seem more like a *razo* than a *vida*, it distinguishes itself from the standard *razo* by the *si fo* of its opening formula and by its failure to make an explicit link with a particular poem.

Jaufre Rudel de Blaja
Vida

> Jaufres Rudels de Blaia si fo mout gentils hom, princes de Blaia. Et enamoret se de la comtessa de Tripol, ses vezer, per lo ben qu'el n'auzi dire als pelerins que venguen d'Antiocha. E fez de leis mains vers ab bons sons, ab paubres motz. E per voluntat de leis vezer, et se croset e se mes en mar, e pres lo malautia en la nau, e fo condug a Tripol, en un alberc, per mort. E fo fait saber a la comtessa et ella venc ad el, al son leit e pres lo antre sos bratz. E saup qu'ella era la comtessa, e mantenent recobret l'auzir e·l flairar, e lauzet Dieu, que l'avia la vida sostenguda tro qu'el l'agues vista; et enaissi el mori entre sos bratz. Et ella lo fez a gran honor sepellir en la maison del Temple; e pois, en aquel dia, ella se rendet morga, per la dolor qu'ella n'ac de la mort de lui.

The *exordium*, while recognizably that of the *vida*, has been significantly modified. The standard pattern "____ de ____ si fo de ____ e fo ____ hom" appears here in abbreviated form: "____ de ____ si fo ____ hom."

Geographical information has likewise been reduced. *Blaia*, the only place name mentioned in the opening statement, occurs twice—once as an epithet with "Jaufres Rudels" and again as part of his title, "princes de Blaia." In both instances, though, *Blaia* acts less as a topographical indicator than as a convenient means of identifying the story's central figure. In describing Jaufré as "gentils," the biographer tells us very little, since several other troubadours are characterized by their biographers in the same way; however, when the author of this *vida* intensifies the adjective *gentils* by *mout*, he sets Jaufré Rudel in a class by himself, for no other troubadour is portrayed in the *vidas* in quite these terms.[21] The biographer further elevates this poet by calling him "princes de Blaia." Whether or not Jaufré Rudel was really a prince remains an unsettled question,[22] but one of no consequence to the present study. What matters, rather, for us is the effect intended by the biographer in conferring such a title. With "mout gentils" and "princes de Blaia," the author of the *vida* encourages his audience to anticipate the portrayal of a highly exalted figure. After these few introductory remarks, the narrative proper begins, the verb "enamoret se" supplying the generative kernel out of which the *vida* develops.

This *vida*, in contrast to Guiraut's and Arnaut's, is articulated almost entirely in the third-person preterite. To posit that everything after the exordial formula acts as a vital link in an ordered chain of events is for the most part merely to state the obvious. There are, however, two places in the account where the narrative aspect of what is stated is not immediately apparent. For example, with the reference to Jaufré Rudel's verses we might be tempted to say that the *vida* has given itself over to a moment of non-narrative literary criticism, but it is important to realize that we are still in the past tense of narration (*fez*) and that the beloved woman is still very much the focus of the poet's activity (*fez de leis*). Furthermore, the placement of this sentence in the heart of the *vida* stresses its narrative over its critical function. The previous sentence reported that Jaufré fell in love with the Countess sight unseen because of what he had heard about her through returning pilgrims. The following sentence goes on to say that the troubadour set out in search of the object of his desire. In this context, the intent of the statement about the poet's versemaking has to do more with connecting the songs to the Countess than with evaluating their literary worth. Hence, while both of the other *vidas* we have studied make comments about the poet's works in the present tense, remarks which do indeed interrupt the narrative flow, the emphasis of the statement about versemaking in this *vida* is on the past act, the "historical" event of composing poems. The thread of the story thus far can be traced as follows: 1) The prince of Blaya fell in love with an unknown woman; 2) he created poems about her; 3) not satisfied, he went on a quest in order that he might see her face-to-face. The verses, then, represent above all a first and inadequate move toward the troubadour's goal of union with the Countess. Of course, one cannot deny that "ab bons sons ab paubres motz" involves at least secondarily a critical commentary on Jaufré's work, but exactly what is meant by *paubres motz* has been a subject of much debate.[23] Many scholars interpret this as a reference to Jaufré Rudel's deliberate choice of the *trobar leu* or "simple style." And yet I cannot help wondering if new light might not be shed on the ambiguous term *paubres* by considering it in its rightful narrative context. Troubadour songs express love. In the view of the biographer, Jaufré's experience of love *ses vezer* "sight unseen" was not enough. The fact that the *motz* are *paubres* may, then, be the natural product of this *amor de lonh*. The *sons*, however, as a function of the technical skill of their inventor and not of his personal experience, would not necessarily be affected by the incomplete nature of his love. Consequently, the *sons* may well be *bons*, but the *motz* can only be *paubres* under the circumstances.

On the basis of Jaufré's changing grammatical function, the *vida* can be divided into four parts. The poet plays an ambivalent role alternating between active initiator and passive recipient of the actions set forth. At the beginning of the text the troubadour is the enterprising subject who *enamoret se, auzi dir, fez, se croset,* and *mes*. Thereupon the direction of the action shifts, and the poet becomes the object of forces beyond himself: "malautia lo pres," "fo condug," "(ella) venc ad el," "(ella) pres lo." At this point the dying poet regains his strength long enough to reassume an active role as the subject of the verbs *saup, recobret, lauzet, agues vista, mori*. Upon the death of the poet, the Countess takes up the instigative role. It is she who at the end of the biographical account *fez, se rendet,* and *ac*. The grammatical shifting of the poet from subject to object is consistent with the nature of the experience being revealed, for this *vida* tells of how love-from-afar becomes reciprocal. Every gesture of the troubadour is executed for the Countess, and eventually her deeds are performed for him. The poet having been properly buried and the Countess having entered a convent, the *I-K* account ends, without any mention of the fact that there are poems to follow.[24] How then is this sealed-off *vida* related to the *cansos* which come after it?

This whole legend about Jaufré Rudel can be understood as an expansion of an image drawn from the famous *canso, Lanquan li jorn*:

> Ai! car me fos lai peleris
> Si que mos fustz e mos tapis
> Fos pels sieus bels huoills remiratz![25]

These verses provide the essential elements upon which the *vida* is constructed: an initial desire ("Ai! car..."), a protagonist ("me"), a willful transformation of self ("fos peleris"), a spatial displacement ("lai"), and a projected realization of the poet's dream ("fos remiratz"). But, whereas a lyric poem can, through metaphor, compress a whole story into a single image, prose must string things out, so to speak, metonymically.[26] Thus, the *canso*'s image of a pilgrim in a distant land is rendered in the *vida* as the story of a man who, for love, became a pilgrim and journeyed to a foreign land. In the expansion of the poem's fanciful image into narrative prose, the two subjunctives of *Lanquan* ("fos," "fos remiratz") are replaced in the *vida* by a series of verbs in the indicative mood ("se croset," "se mes," "pres," "saup," "era," "recobret," "lauzet," "avia sostenguda," "mori"). What the *canso* states succinctly as "fos remiratz," the *vida* breaks down into three successive stages built around a prosaic analogue of *remirar*, i.e. *vezer*. At the beginning of the episode Jaufré's love is conceived "ses vezer," that is, without seeing the Countess. He then goes off "per voluntat de leis vezer." Finally, dying in the arms of his beloved, he thanks God for having kept him alive "tro qu'el agues vista." The infinitive form of *vezer* represents the abstract notion of sight with its potential actualization in the future, whereas *vista* refers to an act of seeing which has already been accomplished. Thus, when *vezer* becomes *vista*, the troubadour's quest is over, and he dies rewarded. All three states of *vezer* occurring in the narrative exist in the single inflected verb of the poetic image, *fos remiratz*. As an imperfect subjunctive, *fos remiratz* expresses simultaneously unreality, longing, and pastness, which are communicated in the *vida* by *ses vezer, per vezer,* and *agues vista,* respectively.

Recognizing that Jaufré's biography is generated by an image extracted from the inner portion of a *canso* helps explain the difference in tone between this *vida* and the more typical ones treated above. Most *vidas* and *razos* that derive from specific songs tend to take their information from the first and/or last stanzas, the thresholds across which we are just entering into, or just emerging from, the lyric world.[27] However, the *vida* for Jaufré

Rudel, coming as it does from one of the middle stanzas of *Lanquan*, transposes into prose the peak of the lyric experience. Despite the *vida*'s obvious dependence on *Lanquan*, the biographer makes no explicit mention of the poem; consequently when the *vida* ends, the jump from the past with the death of the poet to the present with the invocation of spring which launches the song seems considerable. It is, however, to some degree appropriate that there be discontinuity between the closing lines of the *vida* and the opening verses of *Lanquan*. Since the poem is about separation and distance, the author of the *vida* does not want to move us too close to the poetic text. When the *canso* begins, we are at one and the same time inside the poem and at a distance from it—victims as it were of the basic *amor de lonh* antithesis of intimacy in distance and distance in intimacy.

Like many other *vidas*, this one for Jaufré Rudel ends at a terminal point in the poet's life. The two protagonists have each taken a final step, the troubadour by dying and the Countess by becoming a nun. Although the very ultimacy of this conclusion may have precluded the invention of further episodes, one must beware of speculation because there is always the possibility that there once existed *razos* which have since been lost. One must remember that the lack of *razos* for Jaufré Rudel might be as much a function of the paucity of surviving songs, which suggests a small opus, as of the conclusive note on which the *vida* stops.

Each of the three texts examined illustrates a different way in which the *vida* may be linked to the poems of a troubadour. In the case of Guiraut de Borneill, the biography concludes by announcing that a sizable corpus of songs is to follow, without specifying which ones they are; the *vida* for Arnaut Daniel leads explicitly into the *tornada* of a particular *canso*, but with implications for all of his pieces, while the account for Jaufré Rudel finishes with no mention that *cansos* are to come. There is also quite a contrast in the kinds of life associated with these three troubadours: Guiraut appears as an assiduous poet-scholar, Arnaut as an ambitious poet-performer, and Jaufré as a princely poet-lover.

A general survey of the *vidas* reveals that even those features which we regard as characteristic traits are by no means constant. We have, for instance, cited the formula "troubadour's name *si fo de* + place name" as the standard *exordium*; an actual count, however, shows that barely more than half of the *vidas* in *I* and *K* (47 out of 87) begin in this manner.[28] Furthermore, there is a wide range of possibilities covered by the category "place name," including everything from a precise toponym to *un borc, la ciutat, l'encontrada*, and *l'evesquat*.[29] Almost as common as the "_____ *si fo de* + place name" exordial paradigm is "_____ *si fo* + predicate nominative." Thirty-seven *vidas* commence in this way, and the substantives which attach themselves to *si fo* are distributed among 7 *joglars*, 6 *castellans*, 6 *cavalliers*, 3 *gentils hom*, 3 *paubres cavalliers*, 2 *bars*, 1 *coms*, 1 *clers*, 1 *borges*, 1 *cantaire*, 4 *fills*, 1 *moiller*, and 1 *major cortes*.[30]

Our generalizations about closure in the *vidas* likewise require some qualification. The stopping places which the *vidas* may contrive fall into various groups. Death is the most frequent resolution. Nineteen *vidas* end with the end of the poet's life. Seventeen of these refer to a natural death, but the next to the last *vida* in *I-K* culminates in the murder of its protagonist, Guillem de Berguedan.[31] Somewhat less final stopping points are reached in other *vidas*: Two end when the troubadour enters a monastery; three conclude when the poet abandons his profession; and three terminate rather more tentatively, when the central figure finds favor at court.[32] Another prevalent method of concluding a *vida* is perhaps better understood as a form of transition than as true closure. Since *vidas* are designed to serve not only as entities unto themselves but also as introductions to poems, an effective technique in structuring such a prose account is to make it move straight into the lyric texts which follow it. In five cases the *vida* (e.g., Arnaut Daniel's) leads explicitly into a specific poem. In fourteen instances the *vida* (e.g., Guiraut de Borneill's) links the narrative to a corpus of songs. Eighteen *vidas*, although not referring expressly to the fact that there are any poems to come, nonetheless prepare the way by focusing their final comments on the troubadour's poetic activity.[33]

The question of verb tenses, too, is less categorical than it may have seemed thus far. Although the preterite is rightly considered the normal tense of the *vida*, we find only twenty-one accounts in *I-K* which use the preterite alone.[34] Most of the texts mix the preterite and the imperfect—some making logical and consistent distinctions between the two tenses, others exercising a freedom which makes explanation according to strictly grammatical criteria unsatisfactory.

There are three situations in the *vidas* where the imperfect appears to be chosen with regularity. First, the imperfect is employed for actions which occur frequently but not continuously. In the *vida* for Guillem Figueira for example, we find at the close of a passage containing eight consecutive preterite forms:

> E s'el vezia bon home de cort venir lai
> on el estava, il n'era tristz e dolenz;
> et ades se penava de lui baissar e de levar
> los arlotz (p. 434).

Secondly, the imperfect is used to distinguish between an action whose effect is permanent and one whose effect cannot endure. It is with this nuance that Gaucelm Faidit's *vida* reports: "cantava peiz d'ome del mon; e fetz molt bos sos e bos motz" (p. 167). Gaucelm's singing, *cantava*, is in the imperfect, but his songmaking, *fetz*, is in the preterite because of the qualitative difference between the products of these two occupations; the songs performed by the troubadour cannot survive the moment of their actualization; however, the songs composed by him can, through the efforts of *jongleurs* and clerks, live on. A third function of the imperfect is to provide background. Not surprisingly, the imperfect tense in this third capacity often occurs in dependent clauses and specifically in the description of secondary characters and events. The opening words of the *vida* for Aimeric de Peguillan illustrate this use of the imperfect:

> N'Aimerics de Peguillan si fo de Tolosa,
> fils d'un borges qu'era mercadiers, que tenia
> draps a vendre (p. 425).

Twice in the *vida* for Bernart de Ventadorn, the troubadour is set off from supporting characters by, among other things, a play of preterite and imperfect verbs. Bernart contrasts thus with his father:

> Hom fo de paubra generacion, fils d'un sirven
> qu'era forniers qu'esquadava lo forn a coszer
> lo pan del castel (p. 20).

Later in the same *vida* the troubadour's position of prominence is reaffirmed by his preterite as opposed to the Duchess of Normandy's imperfect:

> E si s'en anet a la duchesa de Normandia qu'era
> joves. . .e s'entendia en pretz. . .(pp. 20-21).

Finally there are some *vidas* where it seems less important to account for each instance of the imperfect than to sense in a general way how it serves to thicken an otherwise flat account. Take, for example, the short *vida* for Lanfranc Cigala:

> En Lanfranc Cigalla si fo de la ciutat de Genoa.
> Gentils hom e savis fo. E fo jutges e cavalliers,
> mas vida de juge menava. Et era grans amadors; et
> entendia se en trobar e fo bon trobador e fes
> mantas bonas chansos e trobava volontiers de Dieu. . . (p. 569).

The distribution of tenses in this text—3 preterites, 3 imperfects, 2 preterites, and 1 imperfect—shows the extent to which the imperfect can be worked into the very weave of the narrative fabric. As for other tenses, many *vidas* contain at least one instance of the present, and a few even go so far as to use the future. Present and future tenses, however, are normally confined to the ends of *vidas*. Consequently, far from disrupting the pastness of the account, they simply ease the transition from the narrative realm of the *vida* to the lyric universe of the poems.

III. *Razos*: The Prose of the Poetic Experience

The word *razo* (<Latin RATIONE [M]) is deeply embedded in the troubadour lyric from the earliest *vers* and *cansos*. Like many other common terms in Old Provençal this one word covers a whole range of meanings that include "reason," "theme," "subject," "argument," "matter," "speech," "talk," "right," "justice," "good sense," "gloss," and "story."[1] Exactly when and how *razo* came to designate a specific prose genre is difficult to ascertain. Nevertheless, the potential for such an application of the word is built into the original concept of *razo* as it figures variously throughout the lyric tradition.

A simple example of how the word *razo* is used in the lyric occurs in a song by Bernart de Ventadorn, where he states: "me dis en razo plana,"[2] *razo* clearly being "articulated language," "words," "speech." Marcabru in one of his pair of starling songs begins: "Ges l'estornels non s'oblida,/quant ac la razon auzida,"[3] *razo* in this case indicating the "audible content," or "message," which the bird is to communicate. The word takes on greater complexity in the following verses by Bernart de Ventadorn:

> Domna, a prezen amat
> autrui, e me a celat,
> si qu'eu n'aya tot lo pro
> et el la bela razo.[4]

Here again *razo* is "speech," or "conversation," a "spoken utterance" which, in contrast to *pro*, represents a gift bestowed publicly.

Razo as a lexical item plays an important role in some of the *sirventes* by Bertran de Born. Consider the verses: "Quar n'ai razo tan novela e tan granda/Del jove rei..."[5] *Razo* in this context stands for the express "subject" of the *sirventes* and implies the "motivation" which first gave rise to the song. Though this instance of *razo* hints at a certain interiority, the concept remains tightly bound to the world of external events, for it was the well-known fact of the Young King's death which provoked the *razo* behind the *sirventes* in question. *Razo* figures interestingly in the following verses from another *sirventes* by Bertran de Born:

> Mon chan fenisc ab dol et ab maltraire
> per totz temps mais e·l tenh per remasut,
> quar ma razo e mon gauch ai perdut
> e·l melhor rei que anc nasques de maire.[6]

In these verses *razo* is once more the "motivation" behind the poem. But here Bertran enlarges the meaning of *razo* by setting it in conjunction with *gauch* "joy." This pairing of *razo* and *gauch* calls to mind Charles Singleton's discussion, *An Essay on the 'Vita Nuova'* (Cambridge, Mass., 1949), of the fundamental duality of the medieval lyric. According to him, a poem "speaks first of all to the senses. But *intus*, further in, a poem will be found to speak to the reason" (p. 47). The *razo/gauch* couple exposes the basic lyric dichotomy between what is felt and what is understood, between the senses and reason. Furthermore, the *razo/gauch* tension characterizes not only the creative act of the poet but also the re-creative act of the listener. The song, as a verbal expression of the poetic consciousness, transfers this dialectic from the poet to his audience. Indeed, the *razo/gauch* opposition permeates an area vaster by far than the lyric: It affects all of medieval aesthetic. To quote Singleton again: "The concept of the intelligible enclosed in the sensible is fundamental for medieval exegesis and aesthetic" (p. 135).

Marcabru's use of *razo* in *Per savi·l tenc ses doptanssa* contributes even greater complexity to the already heavily laden meaning of the term. The first four verses of the poem proceed thus:

> Per savi·l tenc ses doptanssa
> cel qui de mon chant devina
> so que chascus motz declina,
> si cum la razos despleia...[7]

This *razo* indicates the "analyzable part" of the poem. It refers to an "intelligible unit of meaning" more comprehensive than the individual word. It connotes large syntactical and thematic patterns which, because they have been rationally assembled, may be just as rationally disassembled.

Jaufré Rudel uses *razo* quite suggestively in a song which begins:

> No sap chantar qui so non di
> Ni vers trobar qui motz no fa
> Ni conois de rima co·s va
> Si razo non enten en si.[8]

In this situation *razo* comes to light as the "controlling idea" of the poetic composition. Initially perceptible only to the creative mind, it determines the direction, or pattern ("co·s va") which the poem as a whole will pursue. So, *razo* in the troubadour lyric tradition, depending on its specific context, can refer to "talk," "motivation," or "complex arrangements of words."

The evolution from the lyric use of *razo* to the prose genre called the *razo* may initially have been oral, as *jongleurs* took to prefacing the songs they were about to perform with a spoken paraphrase of what they would shortly be singing, or the process may have been more strictly literary, as clerks, already in the habit of glossing what they copied, began to apply this same exegetical principle to vernacular poetry. Then again, *razos* may have their roots in a soil conducive to a mixture of these oral and written traditions. At any rate, the choice of the word *razo* to name this new kind of vernacular prose composition seems natural, given the wealth of fitting connotations which this word has acquired in filtering down through the lyric. Let us turn then to the study of two specific *razos*, the one about Bertran de Born and the other about Peire Vidal.

Razo of Poem 80.12
(for Bertran de Born)

Bertrans de Born si era drutz d'une domna gentil e jove e fort prezada, et avia non ma domna Maeuz de Montaingnac, moiller d'En Talairan, qu'era fraire del comte de Peiregors; et ella era filla del vescomte de Torena e seror de ma dompna Maria de Ventadorn e de N'Elis de Monfort. E, segon qu'ell dis en son chantar, ela·l parti de si e·il det comjat, don el fo·n mout tristz e iratz, e fez razo que ja mais no la cobraria, ni autra non trobava que fos tan bella ni tan bona ni tan plazens ni tan enseingnada. E penset, pois qu'el non poiria cobrar neguna que·ill pogues esser egals a la soa domna, si [·s] conseillet qu'el en fezes una en aital guisa qu'el soiseubes de las autras bonas dompnas e bellas de chascuna una beutat o un bel senblan o un bel acuillimen o un avinen parlar o un bel captenemen o un bel gran o un bel taill de persona.

Et enaissi el anet queren a totas las bonas dompnas que chascuna li
dones un d'aquestz dos que m'avetz auzit nomar per restaurar la soa
domna c'avia perduda. Et el sirventes qu'el fetz d'aquesta razon vos
auziretz nommar totas las domnas a las quals el anet querre socors et
ajuda a far la domna soiseubuda. E·l sirventes qu'el fetz d'aquesta razon
si comensa:

Domna, pois de mi no·us cal.[9]

80.12

I   Domna, pois de mi no·us chal
   e partit m avetz de vos
   senes totas ochaisos,
   no sai on m'enquiera,
5   que jamais
   non er per mi tan rics jais
   cobratz, e si del semblan
   no trob domna a mon talan
   que valha voa qu'ai perduda,
10   jamais no volh aver druda.

II   Puois no·us posc trobar egal,
   que fos tan bela ni pros,
   ni sos rics corps tan joios,
   de tan bela tiera
15   ni tan gais,
   ni sos rics pretz tan verais,
   irai per tot achaptan
   de chascuna un bel semblan
   per far domna soisseubuda,
20   tro vos me siatz renduda.

III   Frescha color natural
   pren, bels Cembelis, de vos
   e·l douz esgart amoros,
   e fatz gran sobriera
25   quar rei lais,

	qu'anc res de be no·us sofrais.
	Mi donz n'Aelis deman
	son adreit parlar gaban:
	quem do a mi donz ajuda,
30	pois non er fada ni muda.

IV
    De Chales la vescomtal
    volh que·m done ad estros
    la gola e·ls mas amdos.
    Pois tenc ma chariera,
35 no·m biais,
    ves Rochachoart m'eslais
    als pels n'Anhes que·m dara·n,
    qu'Iseutz, la domna Tristan,
    qu'en fo per tot mentauguda,
40 no·ls ac tan bels a saubuda.

V
    N'Audiartz, si be·m vol mal,
    volh que·m do de sas faissos,
    que·lh estai gen liazos,
    e quar es entiera,
45 qu'anc no·s frais
    s'amors ni·s vols en biais.
    A mon Melhz-de-be deman
    son adreit, nou cors prezan,
    de que par a la veguda,
50 la fassa bo tener nuda.

VI
    De na Faidid' autretal
    volh sas belas dens en dos,
    l'acolhir e·l gen respos
    don es presentiera
55 dinz son ais.
    Mos Bels Miralh volh que·m lais
    sa gaieza e son bel gran,
    e quar sap son benestan
    far, don es reconoguda,
60 e no s'en chamja ni·s muda.

VII
    Bels Senher, eu no·us quier al
    mas que fos tan cobeitos
    d'aquesta com sui de vos;
    qu'una lechadiera
65 amors nais,

                don mos cors es tan lechais,
                mais volh de vos lo deman
                que autra tener baisan.
                Doncs mi donz per que·m refuda,
     70   pois sap que tan l'ai volguda?

VIII   Papiols, mon Aziman
                m'anaras dir en chantan
                qu'amors es desconoguda
                sai e d'aut bas chazeguda.[10]

    Razo C for Bertran de Born is based on *Domna pois de mi no·us chal*, a rather unusual little poem, which, though lyric, may be summarized like a narrative. Because Bertran's lady does not care for him and has sent him away without any cause, the poet is at a loss as to where to seek a new love. He is certain that he will never again experience such noble joy and that if he cannot find anyone who measures up to his first lady, he wishes to renounce love altogether. Since no one woman can be her equal, he will go about collecting the finest qualities from among the various women that he knows, his goal being to put together a makeshift lady whose image he can possess until his only true love is restored to him. Taking stock of his women-friends and their features, he selects the coloring and sweet look of Cembelis, the speech of Aelis, the throat and hands of the Viscountess of Chalais, the exquisite tresses of Anhes, the general manner of Audiart, the body of *Melhz-de-be*, the teeth and greeting of Faidida, and the gaiety and pleasing size of *Bels Miralhz*. With the completed image before him, Bertran now addresses himself to his beloved lady, calling her by the *senhal* "Bels Senher"; he asks nothing of her except that he might desire her imaginary counterpart as much as he does her. But alas, the mere request of a kiss from the unattainable *Bels Senher* is more to be desired than actually kissing anybody else, especially this fabricated substitute. The poem proper concludes with a rhetorical question summarizing the utter frustration of the poet: "Why does my lady refuse me when she knows how much I have longed for her?" The *tornada* then sends the song on its way to a friend Aziman via the *jongleur* Papiol, and the final two verses offer a pithy commentary on the state of *fin'amors*: perfect love goes unrecognized where it still exists and, for the most part, it has fallen to a low and disreputable condition.

    Significantly *Domna* is not called a *canso*, but rather a *sirventes*.[11] The *sirventes* is a poem identical to the *canso* in form, yet differing radically from it in subject matter. While the *canso* deals exclusively with love, the *sirventes* deals with other matters—morals, satire, or judgments on men and issues of the day; more often than not, its slant is political. Hence, the *sirventes* is much more intimately involved with the historical reality of twelfth-century Midi culture than the largely atemporal, introspective *canso* could ever be. A problem arises, though, when we try to fit this *sirventes* by Bertran de Born into the general definition of the genre because this song concerns unrequited love and, thus, would appear to emulate the content as well as the form of the typical *canso*. Why, then, should *Domna pois* be considered a *sirventes* at all?

Although there may be many other arguments for *Domna*'s classification as a *sirventes*, let us look briefly at two of the more persuasive ones. In the first place, the private world of the *canso*, where the troubadour has eyes only for his particular lady, has been transformed into a world filled with a multitude of beautiful females, of whom the poet is very much aware. Granted, the one that he really adores occupies a class by herself and is, in a sense, beyond comparison; nevertheless, she does not exist in a vacuum. She is surrounded by other lovely women, each of whom has some outstanding feature that strikes the poet as perfect. Although the beloved lady bears only the pseudonym *Bels Senher*, some of the women who become, so to speak, members of the "synthetic lady" are named explicitly—Aelis, the Viscountess of Chalais, Anhes and Faidida. Thus, the exclusive "I"/"you" universe of the *canso* has expanded to take in identifiable, third-person figures from the outside world.

In the second place, this *sirventes*, perhaps because of its close link with the external world, reflects a conception of love quite distinct from what we find in the typical *canso*. In the *canso* it is uniquely through the contemplation of a particular lady that the poet knows love. He does not analyze the woman's various members; indeed, one almost has the feeling that he does not see them and that he perceives the lady, rather, as the personification of abstract love itself. The *canso*, then, considers the woman as a perfect whole; it may, of course, on occasion single out one or more of her features, but these traits are rarely detached from their ensemble. Bernart de Ventadorn recalls, for example, the treacherous eyes of his lady in the verse, "li seu belh olh traïdor,"[12] and in another song this same poet describes separately the body and face of his ideal woman:

> Ai, bon'amors encobida,
> cors be faihz, delgatz e plas!
> Ai, frescha charn colorida.[13]

Guiraut de Borneill, too, elaborates on the charms of his lady's body: "Tan es sos cors gais et isneus/e complitz de belas colors."[14] Arnaut Daniel points out the sweetness of his lady's face: "Doussa car', a/totz aips volgutz,"[15] and in the celebrated *Eu son Arnautz* song, he comments in particular on the hair and body of his beloved:

> E qan remir sa crin saura
> e·l cors q'es grailet e nou
> mais l'am que qi·m des Luserna.[16]

Such references to separate features are infrequent, however, in the *canso* tradition and represent less an attempt to isolate or systematize the components of the woman's beauty than an effort to capture in miniature the essence of her full appeal. The lyric's synecdochal use of the various parts of the body—eyes, face, hair, etc.—cannot be too strongly stressed. We should keep in mind also that "body" may not mean corporeal body at all. In Old Provençal *mos cors* is a periphrasis for the first-person pronoun *eu*; similarly, *sos cors* and *lo cors* might be merely alternative ways of saying "she."[17] Thus, it appears that the process described in this *sirventes* whereby Bertran dismembers a number of less-than-perfect women in order to construct one perfect one contradicts the *canso*'s understanding of perfection, which lies in *mesura*—unity and proportion—and never in the extravagant concatenation of disjointed parts.[18]

Having considered what makes *Domna* a *sirventes*, we move to the issue of what makes this particular *sirventes* convenient for development into a *razo*. The most obvious point is that the poem tells us quite plainly why it was composed: Bertran's lady has rejected him, and the grieving poet resolves to replace her with an image. Hence, the *jongleur* or clerk, or whoever it was, found a ready-made *razo* in the poetic text; he was obliged to resort neither to idle speculation nor to his knowledge of Bertran as an historical personage in order to assign a reason for the invention of this song. Another aspect of *Domna* which suits it admirably for transformation into a *razo* is that the entire poem is constructed around a single well-developed image. Although there is no definite time sequence involved in the poet's gathering together of qualities, the multiple stages which constitute this extended image adapt themselves quite well to a linear presentation in prose.

A third characteristic of this poem which could attract the prospective biographer is its reference to real people. By naming documentable figures, the *sirventes* provides good raw material for building a concrete, presumably "factual" prose account. This is not to imply, however, that the poem limits itself to real people with real names. Alongside the historical women we find the legendary Iseut, and we discover, too, that some veritable men and women are designated by fictitious names or *senhals—Cembelis, Audiart, Melhz-de-be, Bels Miralhz, Bels Senher, Aziman*. Thus the composer of the *razo* may have found in *Domna* just the right blend of fact and fiction to quicken his creative urge.[19]

Finally, *Domna*'s piecemeal construction of the ideal woman is analogous to the generic process which brings *vidas* and *razos* into being. The biographers, like Bertran in *Domna*, perceived the *fin' amors* paradigm as an assortment of fragments from which they attempted to shape a coherent whole. Bertran says to his *jongleur*, Papiol, that "amors es desconoguda/sai e d'aut bas chazeguda" (vv. 73-74). And, certainly, it was also the case for the composers of the *vidas* and *razos* that the perfect love celebrated in the *cansos* seemed shattered. Possibly the author of the *razo* found in this *sirventes* a striving after the same model of perfection which he was seeking to reinstate.

Let us look, then, at the *razo* itself, remembering all the while the nature of the poem from which it evolves. The *razo* for Bertran's poem 80.12 announces immediately the genre to which it belongs. There are two other *razos* which begin with this same formula of "troubadour's name *si era drutz*," one being *Razo D* for Bertran de Born and the other, the *razo* for the Dalfin d'Alvergne.[20] And though the occurrence of the *exordium* "si era drutz" in three texts may seem an inadequate basis for calling it a "pattern," there is an undeniable tendency for *razos* to begin by focusing on the poet's role as lover. This *exordium* establishes the text as a *razo* also by its use of the imperfect tense. Unlike the *vidas*, which always start abruptly in the preterite with the fact of the troubadour's existence, the *razos* characteristically commence *in medias res*. They catch the troubadour at a transitional moment between episodes in his life. By choosing the imperfect for the first few verbs of his account (*era, avia, era, era*), the composer of the *razo* provides the background against which he will develop his narrative.

While Bertran's lady remains veiled in mystery in the *sirventes*, where she is addressed in terms no more open than *Bels Senher*, she loses any such vagueness in the *razo*, where she goes by her proper name, Maheut de Montagnac. Moreover, if the name Maheut should happen not to mean anything to us, the author of the *razo* eliminates any possible uncertainty about who she is by telling us who her husband, brother-in-law, father and siblings are. With this rather cumbersome genealogical information out of the way, the narrative proper begins.

Tense shifts from the imperfect to the preterite and, concommitantly, the focus switches from background to action.[21] The *razo* introduces the narrative section with "segon qu'el dis en son chantar," a clause which establishes Bertran's poetry as the authority for the events which are about to unfold. Up to this point the facts of the account have been drawn from sources outside the *sirventes*. With "segon. . .," however, the perspective changes, and from here on the standard of truth will not be external reality so much as the poem.

The sentence which begins with "E segon" corresponds to the first stanza of the poem. If we compare the words of the prose to those of the poetry, we discover varying degrees of fidelity to the *sirventes*. The prose statement "ela·l parti de si" reproduces as nearly as possible the verse which says, "e partit m'avetz de vos." The "I"/"you" configuration in the lyric naturally becomes a "he"/"she" set-up in the prose commentary. The poem's verb *partir*, employed in an active sense, is retained by the prose. The tense of *partir* changes, as we might expect, in accordance with the different temporal schemes which characterize the two genres in question. The *sirventes* uses the *passé composé* to designate a real action which, though performed in the past, continues to have a bearing on the rest of the poem, which is basically in the present. The *razo*, however, puts *partir* in the preterite, just as it does all of the other verbs in the account. By placing *parti* at the head of a chronological chain of past events, the composer of the *razo* endows the verb with a causative significance similar to the one given to it by the poet when he made it a present perfect in relation to the present tense of the poem as a whole. As a general rule it seems that relative chronology in a lyric situation must be conveyed through a modification of tense, whereas anteriority in a prose account may be shown simply by listing events, all of which are in the same tense.

The description of the poet's emotional state undergoes an interesting evolution between the *sirventes* and the *razo*. The distraught poet does not give names to the emotions he feels. He says only that he does not know where to turn in search of a new love ("no sai on m'enquiera"), but the composer of the *razo*, looking at the poet from the vantage point of an outsider, pronounces him *tristz* and *iratz*. The expression *fez razo*, an innovation in the prose account, serves the double purpose of reminding us of the genre within which we are operating (the *razo*) and of showing there to be a rational basis for the poet's decisions, which, in the poem, are prompted purely by irrational instinct ("no sai").

Both the *sirventes* and the *razo* employ an inflected form of the verb *cobrar*; the future tense of it in the poem makes the predictable shift to the conditional in the prose. What is significant, though, is that the object of the verb is different in the two genres. In *Domna* the thing which will not be recovered is joy, while in the *razo* it is the lady. This change illustrates the more concrete nature of the prose commentary, where the flesh-and-blood woman replaces impalpable euphoria as the object of the poet's quest.

The *razo* follows the *sirventes* in its choice of the verb *trobar*, but, while the poet explains in general terms that he is looking for a woman who, to his way of thinking ("a mon talan"), is as worthy as the one who rejected him, the prose writer enumerates the particular aspects in which the new woman is expected to compare. Maheut's surrogate must be just as *bella, bona, plazens* and *ensegnada* as she. *Razo C*'s more extensive specifications at this early point as to the person who could match Bertran's lady reflect, I believe, the disparity in the way that a lyric poem and a biography initially project the woman. The *canso* perceives first and foremost the whole being, and although *Domna* is technically not a *canso* but a *sirventes*, it is not until the second stanza that it deviates from the standard *canso* paradigm. Consequently, the opening stanza of Bertran's poem portrays the lady in the same nonspecific terms as would a regular *canso*. The *razo*, however, with its less ethereal, more empirical perspective, recognizes immediately the various parts and then sees the whole as a product of their coincidence. The first stanza of the poem ends with the poet's resolve not to take another *druda* "mistress." Though the prose account offers no statement equivalent to this (except, of course, in the poem itself, which completes the *razo*), it does retain the concept of *druderia* "courting" in its opening comment about Bertran as a *drutz*.

The sentence beginning "E penset..." transposes into narrative terms the situation described in stanza II of the *sirventes*. The poem, now just beginning to display its non-*canso* colors, breaks down the perfection of the woman into a number of distinct attributes. The *razo*, too, enumerates qualities, not specifically those Maheut possesses but those which Bertran will find among other women—*beutat, semblan, accuillimen, parlar, captenemen, gran* and *taill.* The expressions *e penset. . .que* and *si·s conseillet. . .qu'*, which the composer of the *razo* tacks onto the front of the clauses of this sentence, emphasize the rational nature of the troubadour, a quality already suggested by the phrase *fez razo.* Terms such as these, which hint at the thought process behind the poet's creative act, help make the *razo* something other than a simple résumé of the content of the poem and render it, instead, a commentary. The clause "pois qu'el non poiria cobrar neguna que ill pogues esser egals a la soa domna" reproduces with very little adjustment the first verse of the *sirventes'* second stanza: "Puois no·us posc trobar egal." The one significant modification is that where the poem has *trobar*, the *razo* opts for *cobrar*. In changing *trobar* to *cobrar*, the composer of the *razo* replaces a verb which has unavoidable poetic overtones by a more prosaic one.

The "E penset" sentence preserves three important words which testify to the close relationship between this statement in prose and *Domna's* second stanza. These are *egals, soiseubes,* and *semblan. Soiseubar*, which is obviously the key word in both the *sirventes* and the *razo*, occurs in the past participle in verse and in the subjunctive in prose. Since in lyric poetry there is no discrepancy between the conceptualization and the realization of a goal, the woman is as good as *soisseubuda* before the image ever works itself out in concrete terms. In the *razo*, on the contrary, a completed picture emerges only with time. At this point in the narrative the project of *soiseubar* exists only in a virtual state as conveyed by the subjunctive *soiseubes*.

The sentence which starts "Et enaissi. . ." handles in a general way material drawn from Stanzas II through VII. Although the previous sentence of the narrative also treats information based on Stanza II, this one carries matters matters a step farther. In the "E penset. . ." sentence Bertran had the idea for the "synthetic lady," but in this new sentence he actually undertakes the work of assembling her. While the composer of the *razo* cuts the story off here, the poet, in Stanzas III through VII of the *sirventes*, will go on to furnish specific details about what features are taken and from whom. Consequently, the "synthetic lady" in prose is devoid of the coloring, sweet look, throat, hands, hair, teeth, and gaiety with which her poetic counterpart is so generously endowed. Indeed, the composer of the *razo* does not bother to list features at all in this sentence but merely has us recall the traits which he tells us he has already singled out. In referring to himself, "que m'avetz auzit nomar," the author of the *razo* becomes his own authority. We shall return shortly to the notion of the biographer as authority when we consider the various points of view in the *razo*, but for the moment let us remark only on the significance of the *passé composé* "avetz auzit." As indicated in the first chapter, the *passé composé* places us in a temporal environment that sets the *razo* off from the *vida*. The *vida*, on the one hand, is largely oblivious to the time of its own performance. It looks back to the troubadour and focuses almost exclusively on the distant past in which he lived and worked. The *razo*, on the other hand, has a more complex orientation that accommodates not only the distant past in which the troubadour first conceived his poem but also the immediate past in which the composer of the *razo* in progress has been recounting the story behind that poem. It is the *passé composé* which serves to communicate this second past time.

The next phrase is introduced by "per restaurar," an infinitive which does not come from the poem but which reflects, rather, a specific concern of the *vidas* and *razos*. A glance at the biographies reveals that the actual word *restaurar* does not occur very frequently; nevertheless, the idea which it conveys is virtually ubiquitous. Since the *vidas* and *razos* as a group are seeking to recover the general culture of the troubadours, stories of restoration involving individual troubadours offer uniquely interesting and appropriate material for the biographers.

The words "Et el sirventes," which usher in the next sentence, reinforce the authority given to the poem with the mention of *son chantar* earlier in the account. This sentence also contains the *razo*'s second instance of the word *razo*. Here it means "reason"; previously it occurred as part of the expression *far razo* meaning to "think," or "calculate," and, although in neither context does it refer expressly to the literary genre of that name, it certainly implies it. The clause "vos auziretz nommar" directs our attention away from the *razo* and toward the upcoming poem. Perhaps it seems a strange reversal of things that the poem should be more explicit about names than the prose account, especially if we recall the detailed genealogy by which Maheut was identified at the beginning of the *razo* when a mysterious *senhal* had been all she was given in the poem. We must remember, however, that the poem in question is a *sirventes*, and, though it starts in a manner typical of the *canso*, it soon departs from the *canso* model, the extensive use of names being one of its conspicuous non-*canso* features. Meanwhile, the *razo*, even if one of its characteristic features is a propensity for specific names, has a responsibility as an introduction or prologue not to reveal everything that the poem is about to say. Therefore, it is not inconsistent with our apperceptions about genre to encounter a lyric poem full of names which the *razo* does not repeat.

The phrase in prose "far la domna soiseubuda" is lifted directly from the poem. The past participle *soiseubuda* gives a sense of completeness to the *razo* because where we saw earlier in the account the inflected form *soiseubes*, the occurrence now of the past participle of that same verb suggests that the action has reached an end. That we have come to the moment of closure is evident both by the return to *soiseubar* and also by the verbatim repetition of a whole phrase: "E·l sirventes qu'el fetz d'aquesta razon." By using these words as an opening clause in two successive sentences, the author indicates that the narrative mechanism is slowing down. Indeed, it ceases altogether right after the second appearance of the phrase, when the words *si comensa* break off the narrative and introduce the text of the *sirventes*.

In considering this *razo* as a whole, we note the different points of view adopted by its author throughout the piece. Unlike some of the other *razos, Razo C* for Bertran de Born does not begin with a stated "I" and "you." For the first three sentences the perspective does not differ substantially from what we found to be typical of the *vidas*. There is an omniscient, ostensibly objective author who does not name himself or make any overt references to himself. The sole intrusion of the first-person voice comes toward the end of the account in the formulaic expression: "que m'avetz auzit nomar." With this phrase the author reveals himself in the direct-object pronoun *m'* and refers us to his own words as authority. Although there is no further mention of "I" or "me," the framework of a first-person voice addressing a second-person audience continues to apply. The second person appears again in the expression "vos auziretz nommar," which, of course, complements nicely "que vos m'avetz auzit nomar." The listeners (*vos*) have already heard (*passé composé*) what the "I" (*m'*) of the *razo* has to say, and these same listeners (*vos*) are about to hear (future) what the *sirventes* itself has to say. To summarize: the viewpoint in the *razo* is, so to speak, double. There is the implicit author who re-creates for an implicit audience the situation which presumably engendered the historical event of the poem, and there is the explicit author who speaks directly to his audience and points openly to the present unfolding of the *razo* and to the living text of the poem.

Although I have emphasized how *Razo C* leaves us with a feeling of completeness, there is an equally important sense in which the story of the love between Bertran de Born and Maheut de Montagnac is not finished. Any *razo*, as we know, has a context, not only with respect to a poem, but also with respect to the *vida* and other *razos* for that poem's inventor. In the case of Bertran de Born there are in addition to the *vida* seventeen *razos*, all preserved in the thirteenth-century *Chansonniers I* and *K*. Among these *razos* we find many which have a political orientation, but we also encounter some which share *C*'s preoccupation with love.

Bertran's *vida* tells us very little that would prepare us for his experience as Maheut's lover. It stresses almost exclusively his activities as a petty nobleman and warmonger. Although it mentions in passing that he was a "bons domnejaire," this attribute gets somewhat lost among the other elements of the list in which it occurs: "Bons cavalliers fo e bons guerrers e bons domnejaire e bons trobaire e savis e ben parlanz. . ."

According to Boutière and Schutz, the arrangement of *razos* for Bertran de Born is without significance (pp. 70-71). Perhaps. Nevertheless, it is remarkable that after nine *razos* dealing purely with politics and war, we come upon the series *F, C, D, E, B*, where love, not war, is the dominant issue.[22] The structure of *Razo F* is one of the things which makes one question whether the order of the *razos* is as haphazard as Boutière and Schutz indicate. This *razo*, which marks the dividing line between nine political accounts and four amorous ones, is itself divided between the themes of love and war. Despite its brevity, the *razo* seems disjointed, for it presents two distinct episodes whose only point of contact, besides Bertran himself, is King Richard the Lionhearted. The first part of the narrative, which takes place in the castle of King Richard, tells of the attraction of Bertran for the King's sister. The second part, set on the battlefield where Bertran is serving in Richard's army, explains how the poet-warrior finds himself one winter's day on the verge of starvation and proceeds to invent a *sirventes* about this miserable state of affairs. Thus, this *razo* with its bipartite organization provides an excellent transition between the political *razos* which precede it and the romantic ones which succeed it. It seems unlikely that *F*'s location between the two sorts of *razo* is merely fortuitous. *F*, having introduced us to the notion of Bertran as lover, *C, D, E,* and *B* each recount amorous escapades related to his involvement with Maheut de Montagnac. It would appear, then, that *C* is linked both to a poem and to a loosely coherent narrative sequence.

Just why Bertran inspired so many *razos* remains a puzzle. His unusual popularity may derive in part from the simple fact that he came from Limousin at the time when troubadour activity was at its peak, thus making him a fitting representative of the tradition as a whole. Another contributing factor is undoubtedly the sheer number of poems he composed, thereby providing ample source material for numerous biographies. A third consideration is that many of his poems were *sirventes*, which, as we have seen, lend themselves to prosification. Finally, Bertran, as a petty nobleman and troubadour, epitomized the *fin' amors* culture. An active participant in both the political and poetic developments of the day, he captured the imagination of the thirteenth-century clerks who compiled the *Chansonniers I* and *K*.

In sharp contrast to the *razo* for Bertran de Born stands our second selection, *Razo Bb* for Peire Vidal. Probably dating from the fourteenth century, this story surpasses the first in the elaborateness of its plot and the fineness of its technique. The text as it is preserved in *Chansonnier E* goes as follows:

Razo Bb
(for Peire Vidal)

Peire Vidal—si com ieu vos ai dig—s'entendia en totas las bonas donas e crezia que totas li volguesson be per amor.

E si s'entendia en ma dona N'Alazais, qu'era moiller d'En Barral, lo senhor de Marceilla, lo quals volia meils a Peire Vidal c'az ome del mon, per lo ric trobar e per las ricas folias que Peire Vidal dizia e fazia; e clamavon se abdui "Rainier". E Peire Vidal si era privatz de cort e de cambra d'En Barral, plus c'ome del mon.

En Barrals si sabia be que Peire Vidals se entendia en la moiller, e tenia lo·i a solatz e tuit aquill c'o sabion. E si s'alegrava de las folias qu'el fazia ni dizia, e la dona ho prendia en solatz, si com fazion totas las autras donas en que Peire Vidal s'entendia; e cascuna li dizia plazer e·ill prometia tot so que·ill plagues e qu'el demandava; et el era si savis que tot ho crezia. E quan Peire Vidal se corrosava ab ela, En Barrals fazia ades la patz e·ill fazia prometre tot so qu'el demandava.

E quan venc un dia, Peire Vidal si saup qu'En Barrals s'era levatz e que la dona era tota sola en la cambra. Peire Vidal intra en la cambra e venc s'en al leit de ma dona N'Alazais e troba la dormen. Et agenoilla se davan ella e baiza li la boca. Et ella sentit lo baizar e crezet qu'el fos En Barrals, sos maritz, e rizen ela se levet. E garda e vit qu'el era·l fol de

Peire Vidal; e comenset a cridar e a far gran rumor. E vengron las donzelas de lains, quant ho auziron, e demandaron: "Quez es aiso?" E Peire Vidal s'en issit fugen. E la dona mandet per En Barral e fes li gran reclam de Peire Vidal, que l'avia baizada. E ploran l'en preguet qu'el en degues ades penre venjansa. Et En Barrals, si com valens hom et adregz, si pres lo fait a solatz e comenset a rire et a repenre la moiller, quar ela avia faita rumor d'aiso que·l fols avia fait. Mas el non la·n poc castiar qu'ela non mezes en gran rumor lo fait, e sercan et enqueren lo mal de Peire Vidal; e grans menasas fazia de lui.

Peire Vidal, per paor d'aquest fait, montet en una nau et anet s'en en Genoa; e lai estet tro que pueis passet outra mar ab lo rei Richart. Que·ill fo mes en paor que ma dona N'Alazais li volia far tolre la persona. Lai estet longua sazo e lai fes maintas bonas chansos, recordan del baizar qu'el avia emblat. E dis—en una chanso que dis *Ajostar e lasar*—que de leis non avi' agut negun guizardo,

(364, 2   Mas un petit cordo.
v. 24-28)   Si aigui c'un mati
                Intrei dins sa maiso
                E·ill baizei la lairo
                La boca e·l mento.

Et en autre luec el dis:
(364, 48   Plus onratz fora c'om natz,
v. 25-27)   Si·l bais emblatz me fos datz
                    E gen aquitatz.

Et en autra chanso el dis:
(364, 36   Be·m bat Amors ab las verguas qu'ieu cueill,
v. 13-16)   Car una vetz, en son reial cabdueill,
                L'emblei un bais don tan fort mi sove.
                Ai! c'a mal trai, qui so c'ama no ve!

Aisi estet longua sazo outra mar, que non auzava venir ni tornar en Proensa. En Barrals, que li volia aitan de be com vos aves auzit, si preguet tan sa moiller qu'ela li perdonet lo furt del baizar e lo·i autreget en do. En Barral si mandet per Peire Vidal, e si·ll fes mandar grassia e bona volontat a sa moiller. Et el venc ab gran alegreza a Marceilla, et ab gran alegreza fo reseubutz per En Barral e per ma dona N'Alazais. Et autreget li lo baizar en do qu'el li avia emblat. Don Peire Vidal fes aquesta chanso que ditz:

(364, 37)   Pos tornatz sui en Proensa,
la qual vos auziretz.[23]

Because of the length and complexity of this *razo*, let us concentrate only on those aspects which are pertinent to our study: namely, its manipulation of setting, time, and perspective; its humorous play on the motifs of illusion and reality; its interpretive function with regard to four specific poems; and its relation to the *vida* which precedes it. It would be well to begin by recounting what happens in Peire's delightful escapade.

Peire Vidal, who loved all the noble ladies and fancied them all irresistibly attracted to him, was particularly smitten by Lady Alazais, the wife of his lord and patron, Baral of Marseille. Baral saw that Peire, his favorite troubadour, was enamoured of his wife, but, far from being jealous, Baral condoned and even encouraged the relationship between them because he took the poet for a fool and considered his actions amusing and inconsequential. One day when the "fool" Peire knew that his lord was out and that Alazais was alone in her bedroom, the opportunistic troubadour sneaked into the room, headed straight for the bed where she was asleep, and boldly kissed her on the mouth. The lady awakened instantly and, assuming logically that her husband had been the one to kiss her, laughed in delight. But not for long, for as soon as she had rallied enough to discern that it was not Baral at all but that idiot Peire Vidal, her laughter turned to screams of horror. In the ensuing pandemonium the ladies-in-waiting scurried in, Peire ran out, Alazais yelled for Baral, and, as she cried hysterically, he just laughed. Try as he might, Baral was unable to convince his wife of the harmlessness and humor of the incident. She insisted that the poet should be pursued and properly punished. Peire, fearing these threats to his life, took a boat to Genoa and soon afterward went overseas to the court of King Richard, where he remained for quite some time. He profited from his exile to compose many fine songs commemorating the stolen kiss. Meanwhile, back at Marseille, Baral had been pleading so doggedly with Alazais on Peire's behalf that she finally relented and agreed to pardon the poet for the kiss and to grant it to him as a gift. Joyful then, Baral sent for Peire Vidal, who, upon his return to Provence, was greeted warmly by both his lord and his lady.

Although up to this point in our essay setting, time, and point of view have been treated as more or less distinct categories, we can now understand to what extent the separations between them are arbitrary and even misleading. All three are contained within a single concept—call it space. For, setting is no more than an effort to pinpoint a precise location in space; time is merely a way of conceptualizing movement through space;

and point of view is nothing other than a way of perceiving direction in space. Any space, defined linguistically, involves a locus from which the articulation emanates, be it "I," "you," "he"; an articulated movement, e.g., "sing," "are listening," "kissed"; and a final destination for the articulation, as for example, "you," or "her."[24]

Unarticulated space is, of course, boundless, and while poets and theologians may not be too much bothered by the infinity around them, more down-to-earth man is. Convinced of the importance of human history, contemporary culture and man's capacity to mould the future, the rationalist feels uncomfortable until he has reduced the endlessness of space to a size and shape he can grasp. The ethereal poet and the down-to-earth rationalist are not necessarily incompatible beings. Indeed they may represent opposing aspects of a single mind. Medieval man, as has been pointed out by Georges Poulet in his *Etudes sur le temps humain* (Paris, 1949), was simultaneously conscious of permanence and change, of infinity and finitude. He saw the limits of time and space both as the curse brought upon him by his own material nature and as the blessing which gave him continuity and moved him toward salvation.[25] Different literary genres reflect differently these two impulses in man. Some interesting discriminations can be made based purely on the emphasis which a particular genre lays on one or the other of these tendencies. Lyric poetry confronts infinity head-on. It allows time to move in freely, just as it happens, and lets infinite space define itself solely in relation to its center—the poetic "I." The *razo*, however, is a different matter. It is consonant with the nature of the *razo*, the literary genre whose very name betokens its rational outlook, that time be organized and space be contained. Indeed, what we have in the typical *razo* is two finite spaces, one inside the other.

The "inner" space of the *razo* is the one of which we are first made aware in this text, *Bb*. The opening word "Peire Vidal" not only names a poet but also identifies a whole spatial construct. This proper noun defines a setting, for the troubadour is to be the focal point of the narrative. Because we know that Peire is dead, the mention of his name generates a time, the past. Moreover, because Peire can operate only in the past, we know that his activity involves something or someone other than us; thus, the point of view is strictly third-person. Pure narration, as Benveniste has recently described it, is neatly accommodated by such a system of third-person forms in a simple past tense. The *razos*, however, are not pure narratives and, consequently, act in a variety of ways to expand the limits of the constricting narrative space.

We find in this *razo* for Peire Vidal a three-way movement to increase the dimensions of its primary narrative framework. The first way in which the *razo* broadens its own space involves the manipulation of what, in traditional terminology, would be known as the "setting." The story in *Razo Bb* begins in Marseille; the scene then narrows to the bedroom of Alazais; from there it expands to take in Marseille, Genoa and the English court, and finally it returns to Marseille. Although the narrative both begins and ends at the Court of Lord Baral, there is a lot of space covered in the interim.

The second way in which the *razo* extends its original spatial limits is by its use of superlative expressions. The narrative proper centers around three characters: Peire, Alazais, and Baral. But, by opening up the ends of his specific statements with all-inclusive superlatives, the biographer sets the tight love-triangle into a larger human scheme. In describing Alazais' love for Peire, for instance, the composer of the *razo* reports: "N'Alazais... volia meils a Peire Vidal c'az ome del mon." Similarly, in referring to Baral's admiration for Peire, the composer explains: "Peire Vidal si era privatz, de cort e de cambra d'En Barral plus c'ome del mon." Superlatives are not reserved for the description of how much Alazais and Baral revere the poet; they are also employed in the revelation of how they mock him. We are told that "En Barrals...tenia lo i a solatz e tuit aquill c'o sabion" and, likewise, that "la dona ho prendia en solatz, si com fazion totas las autras donas...." We see, then, that the judgment passed on Peire by Baral and Alazais is shared by courtly society at large. The effect of all these superlatives is to set the individual poet, Peire Vidal, in a public domain and thereby to broaden his appeal.

Though the two kinds of spatial enlargement treated thus far (geographical and human) may cause the narrative framework to bulge out a little at the edges, both of them leave this primary structure essentially intact. There is, however, a third way in which the *razo* increases its space. This last way entails the establishment of a new, more comprehensive framework which shall, for lack of a better term, be designated the "outer space." The outer space is defined by the intrusion into the narrative of an explicit "I" and "you," figures who cannot logically be integrated into the story but who are nonetheless indispensable participants in the complex *razo* scheme.

The so-called intrusion of "I" and "you" is quite literally that. If we go back to the beginning of *Bb*, we recall that the evocation of "Peire Vidal" has laid down the basic narrative space within which the main plot is to unfold. However, no sooner has this inner space been articulated than the biographer interrupts with his timely "si com ieu vos ai dig" which jolts us out of the past of narration and sets us in a temporal sphere which endures even now. Interestingly, this second framework does not obliterate the first: the "I"/"you" structure serves merely to circumscribe the narrative structure generated by the initial "Peire Vidal." Hence two settings, the then-and-there of the troubadour doing something and the here-and-now of the biographer recounting that something to us, both obtain at any given point in the development of this *razo*. Although then-and-there and here-and-now would seem to be non-intersecting, mutually exclusive linguistic possibilities, they find reconciliation generically in the *razo*, where both are continuously operative.

The "I"/"you" configuration, having been set up at the beginning of the *razo*, remains in effect throughout the *razo*'s development, although not expressly mentioned again until near the end when the composer of the *razo* leaves Peire Vidal stranded overseas and relocates the story in Marseille, where Baral, who was extremely fond of Peire, "si com vos aves auzit," was doing all he could to make his wife forgive the poet. The third and final overt reference to "I" and "you" concludes the *razo*: "la qual vos auziretz."

Having seen how the mention of "I" and "you" makes manifest the simultaneous operation of two different spatial cosntructs in the *razo*, let us now consider more specifically how the "I"/"you" point of view does indeed serve to point our view. With "si com ieu vos ai dig" the biographer has us turn toward the past; with "com vos aves auzit" he has us reflect upon the present; and with the closing "si com vos auziretz" he has us look to the future; or to put it into generic terms, he directs our attention to the preceding *vida*, the current *razo* and the upcoming poem, respectively. We must remember, though, that even if the comprehensive "I"/"you" structure can be aimed toward the past or the future, the structure itself is essentially present, and any other tense that the first-person biographer may wish to employ is necesarily defined with reference to his own immutable stand in an ongoing present.

In contrast to the self-consciousness of the outer space, the inner space ignores the necessity of the first-person voice which articulates it. It remains in a past far-removed from us and does not need to define itself in relation to our present. The temporal dimension of the inner space in *Razo Bb* typifies what we find for *razos* in general. A long series of imperfect verbs builds the background. This sequence of imperfects is broken by the preterite *venc*, the standard word employed to inaugurate the narrative proper. Henceforth the narrative works itself out, just as we might have predicted, in the preterite, but for one startling exception...

There is a present tense right at the climax of the story: It is the staccato cry uttered by the flustered ladies-in-waiting. "Quez es aisso?" The terse bit of *oratio* "Quez es aisso?" jars the smoothness of the narrative flow in a fashion analogous to interrupters like "si com ieu vos ai dig" and "com vos aves auzit." This three-word question, which so neatly conveys the chaos wrought by the impetuous troubadour, itself wreaks chaos on our neat *razo* structure. Because the cry does not come from one of the central characters but rather from a chorus of anonymous ladies-in-waiting, the intimate little sin committed by the troubadour in the privacy of his lady's boudoir blows up instantaneously into a full-scale scandal. This use of direct discourse offers another example, then, of how Peire Vidal's *razo* stretches its own narrative space. Moreover, because the disruptive "Quez es aisso?" is in the present tense and represents the words of some person or persons speaking directly to others, it reminds us immediately of the *razo*'s outer structure, in which the biographer addresses us. In fact, we are not unlike the eager ladies, peripheral figures who rush impulsively to the center of excitement and try to participate actively in it. Thus, there is a sense in which "Quez es aisso?", while belonging to the inner space, reflects what is happening in the outer space and suggests a point of convergence for these two frameworks.

Having discovered that space takes in geography, temporality, and viewpoint, we have applied this understanding in our previous remarks on *Razo Bb* for Peire Vidal. Though such an examination may be useful in demonstrating how a specific text operates within the two spaces indigenous to every *razo*, this exercise alone does not do justice to the peculiar appeal of this prose account. Indeed, our serious abstractions about space have practically obscured the captivating frivolity of the text. Let us, then, rectify this misrepresentation of the text by looking at it as the highly comic piece that it is.

The humor in this *razo* derives from the repeated discrepancy between appearance and reality, especially as this disparity is expressed by the juxtaposition of the antonymical verbs *crezer* and *tener/penre en solatz*. We are told that Peire Vidal believed (*crezia*) that all the noble ladies were madly in love with him, but then we learn that not only Alazais but all the other ladies as well took Peire in jest (*en solatz*). We are informed that Lord Baral knew of Peire's feelings for his wife, but that he, like everyone else, took the poet lightly (*a solatz*). All the ladies made Peire fine promises, which, as the biographer states ironically, the troubadour was smart (*savis*) enough to believe (*el crezia*)! Nor was the poet the only one who believed what he should not have. Alazais, awakened by someone's kissing her, thought (*crezet*) that it was her husband. The problem with Baral, however, was the opposite in that he did *not* believe what he should have; consequently, instead of being upset over the poet's audacity or his wife's fallen reputation, he saw the whole thing as a joke ("pres lo fait a solatz").

In addition to the heavily exploited opposition between believing (*crezer*) and disbelieving (*tener en solatz*), other antithetical actions are set against each other with amusing results. For example, the biographer explains that every time the poet had a tiff (*se corrosava*) with Alazais, Baral would jump in and make peace (*fazia la patz*) between them. In a second instance the composer of the *razo* describes how Alazais tearfully (*ploran*) related the mortifying incident to her husband and how he responded by bursting into laughter (*comenset a rire*). And contrasting gestures are funnier still when performed by the same character. Such is the case with the startled Alazais, who one minute was laughing (*rizen*) over what she thought had occurred and the next was screaming (*comenset a cridar*) over what had really taken place.

What happens to Peire would be entertaining no matter who he was, but the fact that he was a poet makes the episode even funnier. Poor Peire! What he believes and what we as outsiders observe are literally worlds apart. He thinks that all the women love him and puts faith in their promises to him. We know better. He perceives reality as he would have it be, not reality as anyone can see that it is. This is a crucial point if we remember what was said above about the nature of poetry, for poetry has the power to give real existence to products of the imagination. Within a poem there is no necessary gap between conceptualization and actualization, since the lyric poem does everything in its power to abolish time. To be specific, the *domna* is as good as *soiseubuda* before the image is ever strung out in concrete steps. But poetry can be taken at its word only in a universe generated according to its own terms. As soon as one begins, as did the biographer for Peire Vidal, to take poetic language at face value in a non-poetic environment, one induces the confrontation of two incongruous systems of truth—the truth of the lyric world versus the truth of the linear world of cause and effect. The composer of *Razo Bb* plays ironically and humorously upon this disparity. Thus, Peire appears as an absurd misfit in the prosaic realm of day-to-day affairs. A true poet, he believes in, and lives out of, his imagination.

Of course, the true and palpable fruits of the poet's imagination are his poems, and this *razo* distinguishes itself by making explicit reference to no less than four *cansos*. All four of the poems cited in the *razo* allude to the stolen kiss, and, hence, all of them are related thematically to the narrative account. It is, however, the first poem (364, 2), *Ajostar*, which contributes the most substantially to the framing of *Razo Bb*. The composer of the *razo* dramatizes, clarifies, and, in clarifying, interprets the state of mind which this *canso* fixates.

364.2

I   Ajostar e lassar
Sai tan gent motz e so,
Que del car ric trobar
No·m ven hom al talo,
5   Quant n'ai bona razo.
Mas auci me aissi
La bella de cui so,
Cum s'ieu fes mespreizo
Vas lieis o tracio.
10   Quant la vi si·m feri
Mon coratge gloto,
Qu'ades poinh el sieu pro,
E no·m fai si mal no.
Mal mi vol e no sai per que,
15   Mas sol quar am lieis mais que me.

II   Assatz par que lonhar
Me volc de sa reio,
Quan passar mi fes mar,
Per qu'ieu la·n ochaizo.
20   Mas no·i ai sospeisso,
Qu'ieu·l servi ab cor fi,

		Tan quan puec a bando,

Tan quan puec a bando,
E no·n aic guizardo,
Mas sol d'un pauc cordo.
25 Si agui qu'un mati
Intrei dins sa maizo
E·lh baiziei a lairo
La boca e·l mento.
So n'ai agut e no mais re
30 E sui totz mortz, si·l plus rete.

III Sospirar e plorar
Mi fai manta sazo,
Qu'alegrar e chantar
Volgra mais, si·l fos bo;
35 Mas cor a de drago,
Qu'a me di mal e ri
Als autres deviro,
E·m fai huelhs de leo:
Per aital faillizo
40 Fes de mi pelegri,
Qu'anc romieus d'orazo
Mais ta forsatz no fo.
E qui·l ver en despo,
Totz hom deu percassar son be,
45 Ans que mals seinhers lo malme.

IV Abrazar e cremar
Mi fai cum fuecs carbo.
Quan l'esgar, tan vei clar
Sos heulhs e sa faisso,
50 Que non sai guerizo,
Si·m cambi ni·m desvi
D'amar liei. Hai baro!
Co·m te en sa preizo
Amors, que Salamo,
55 E Davi atressi
Venquet e·l fort Samso,
E·ls tenc en son grillo,
Qu'anc non ac rezemso
Tro a la mort; e pus mi te,
60 Ad estar m'er a sa merce.

V Esperar e muzar
Mi fai coma Breto,
Qu'anc l'amar ni l'honrar
No·lh mis en contenso.

	65	Ans, si Dieus mi perdo,
		M'en parti de tal qui
		M'agra dat tan ric do,
		Que·l bos reis d'Arago
		For' honratz; e doncs co
	70	Me faidi? Qu'ie·us afi,
		Quan n'aug dir bon resso
		Gaugz entiers mi somo
		Qu'en deia far chanso.
		E doncs pus tan l'am e la cre,
	75	Ja no·i dei trobar mala fe.
VI		Pus pauzar ni finar
		No puesc nulha sazo,
		Retornar et anar
		M'en vuelh ad espero
	80	Entr'Arle e Tolo
		A tapi, quar aqui
		Am mais un pauc cambo,
		Qu'aver sai Lo Daro,
		Ni aver Lo Toro
	85	N'Ibeli: mas frairi
		Fals lauzengier gloto
		M'an moguda tenso
		E lunhat del Peiro,
		E·N Dorgomans no m'au ni·m ve,
	90	Quar mon car Amic part de se.
VII		A mon amic Folco
		Tramet lai ma chanso
		Que la chant en bon loc per me,
		Al tenen on joi vai e ve.
VIII	95	Mal astre Dieus li do,
		Qui·l comte d'Avinho
		Mesclet tan malament ab me,
		per que Na Vierna no·m ve.
IX		Mas a Tripol m'ado,
	100	Que quan l'autre baro
		Caço prez, et el lo rete
		E no·l laissa partir de se.[26]

Let us look at some examples of how *Ajostar* serves as a source for *Razo Bb*. In the song the poet complains that his lady torments him as though he had offended her: "cum s'ieu fes mespreizo/Vas leis o tracio" (vv. 8-9). Did he wrong her or not? The poem with its subjunctive "cum s'ieu fes" deliberately leaves the question unsettled. And a few verses later the poet expresses his ostensible confusion about why his lady seeks to do him harm. According to Peire: "Mal mi vol e no sai per que" (v. 14). Any ambiguity which might reside in the poem's "cum s'ieu fes" and "no sai per que" is, however, dispelled by the *razo*'s treatment of the matter, for in the prose version the poet definitely did offend Alazais and, whether justly or unjustly, it was definitely on account of the stolen kiss that he was being punished. A third spot where *Ajostar* leaves things deliberately vague is vv. 16 and 17, in which the troubadour speaks of his exile. He states: "Assatz par que lonhar/Me volc de sa reio." Now, in the *razo*, it is more than "fairly apparent" that Alazais wanted Peire out of her sight forever. She said as much, publicly and unequivocally:

> Mas el non la·n poc castiar qu'ela non mezes en gran rumor lo fait, e sercan et enqueren lo mal de Peire Vidal; e grans menasas fazia de lui.

She could hardly have been clearer than that! The part of *Ajostar* from which the *razo* derives the major lines of its plot is the passage quoted in the *razo*, vv. 23-29. The *razo* does not allude to the mysterious cord mentioned by the poet; otherwise, though, it reproduces with very little alteration the material contained in these verses. *Un mati* becomes *un dia*, a change which does not appear to be of any particular importance. The first-person *intrei* automatically shifts to the third-person *intra*. *Maizo* turns into a precise *cambra*, and the first-person kiss "baizei. . .la boca" becomes a third-person deed in prose: "baiza. . .la boca."

There are two other instances where the *razo* depends conspicuously on information found in the poem. The poet describes his lady's cruelty to him by saying that she simultaneously "di mal e ri" (v. 36). Because different emotions are not experienced concurrently but, rather, in succession in logical prose, the *razo* breaks down the complex poetic state of anger/glee into two distinct and rationally motivated reactions. The ingenious result of this depoeticization is that the lady, who, in the *canso*, heartlessly curses the poet out of one side of her mouth and laughs out of the other, is depicted in the *razo* first as laughing, then as cursing, with a perceptible pause in between for a conscious shifting of her emotional gear. The final instance to be remarked is the *razo*'s transposition of v. 62. In the *canso* the poet bemoans the fact that his lady makes him wait *coma Breto* "like a Breton." This simile refers to the reputation that the Bretons had of always waiting for King Arthur to return.[27] But the biographer, instead of interpreting *Breto* metaphorically as someone who waits, takes it literally as someone from Britain; therefore, to make Peire wait like a Breton requires shipping him off to Britain, where he can be linked, metonymically at least, with the people who live there. And that explains why in *Razo Bb* Peire goes to the Court of King Richard and waits.

The carrying-over of material from *Ajostar* to *Razo Bb* is facilitated by the fact that this lyric poem has a short "narrative" moment in it. The poetic telling of the stolen kiss takes place in the preterite and is recounted sequentially as *intrei* (I entered) and *baizei* (I kissed). In order to rework these verbs into a *razo*, one need change only their person; their tense and order already conform to a narrative pattern.

The next poem (364, 48), *Tant me platz jois e solatz*,[28] treats the kiss more strictly lyrically than *Ajostar*. The mood of this second *canso* is set by its apostrophes to the exalted lady, before whom the poet humbly begs mercy. Given the poem's overall tone of supplication, it is not surprising to find the kiss couched between two verb forms expressive of desire, a conditional *fora* and a past subjunctive *fos datz, autreyatz*. Apart from the kiss, the only element common to both poem and *razo* is Rainier, the lord to whom Peire in his poem offers words of praise and encouragement. The composer of the *razo* identifies Rainier as Baral of Marseille and shows his influential role in the determination of the troubadour's fate. By recounting Baral's specific efforts on Peire's behalf, the biographer explains why Peire Vidal had good reason to be extolling this noble lord.

The third poem (364, 36), *Plus que·l paubres*,[29] offers yet another perspective on the obsessive kiss. If the first *canso* viewed it in a context of past reality and the second set it in a context of unrealized desire, this poem places the kiss squarely in the present. The poet tells us that love is beating him ("be·m bat Amors" [v. 13]) at this very moment, and though he uses the past tense for the actual theft of the kiss ("imblei un bais" [v. 15]), he immediately returns to the present with *ara mi sove* "now I remember" (v. 15). The meaning here is patent: Through remembering, past can be transformed into present. The *razo* brings out this idea of memory when it reports that during his long exile Peire "fes maintas bonas chansos, recordan del baizar qu'el avia emblat." This sentence not only restates what the song says but also renders explicit a step in the process of preserving past experience that the *canso* takes for granted, for the song does not comment expressly on its own role in the process of memory. Memory alone can convert past to present temporarily, but only poetry can fixate it.

After citing from the three poems the composer of the *razo* resumes the narrative. He draws the information for this final paragraph from the song into which the paragraph leads, *Pus tornatz sui en Proensa* (364, 37).[30] The opening verse of this fourth *canso* authorizes the biographer to conclude that Alazais did eventually forgive the poet. Like *Ajostar, Pus tornatz sui* contains an allusion to the Bretons; in this case, though, the poet makes their waiting for Arthur explicit and, in so doing, limits the possible interpretations that may be placed on the image. The perspective on the kiss in *Pus tornatz sui* differs from what we found in the three previous poems. Not only the kiss but also the approval of it are in the past. The time of waiting is over, and the troubadour has emerged victorious from his exile. *Razo* and poem alike end the story here. The closing stanza of *Pus tornatz* is addressed to Rainier, who was the named recipient of the second poem, too, and who, under his "real" name Baral, has played a key role in the *razo*.

This *razo*'s use of material from four songs illustrates the sophistication of the *razo* as a literary genre, for no matter how one may evaluate the likelihood of the incidents recorded in this and other biographical texts about Peire, one cannot deny that whoever put together *Razo Bb* was quite familiar with Peire Vidal's poems and used them intelligently in the construction of his account. In the case of *Ajostar*, the biographer's knowledge of the song was thorough indeed. His interpretations reflect the down-to-earth literalism of the *razo* mentality, *Breto* being the most obvious case in point here. Furthermore, his transpositions of poetic situations into prose demonstrate yet again for us how prose lays out side by side notions which can be expressed lyrically as a single concept, the best example of this being the *canso*'s portrayal of the lady as simultaneously angry and gleeful while the *razo* shows her experiencing the two feelings in a temporal succession.

Though struck by the unusual abundance of poetic sources upon which *Razo Bb* builds, we are not fully aware of the complexity of this text until we have also considered how it builds on the *vida* for Peire Vidal.[31] This *vida* occurs not only in all the fourteenth-century manuscripts in which we find the *razo*, but in the four extant *vida*-bearing *chansonniers* of the thirteenth century as well. Whether this means that the *vida* predates the *razo* by as much as a century is difficult to determine, nor does it really matter. The crucial point is that the *vida* was unquestionably composed before the *razo* and that the composer of the *razo*, if not himself the author of the *vida*, was at least conscious of the *vida's* existence. The opening words of *Razo Bb* declare its dependence on the *vida*. In saying "si com ieu vos ai dig," the composer of the *razo* refers us to a foregoing narrative. Moreover, it seems evident that this previous account must be the *vida* because the precise information which the author of the *razo* claims to have told us already, "s'entendia en totas las bonas donas," is a verbatim restatement of the *vida*'s "E si entendia en totas las bonas dompnas. . . ." Such a reference within a *razo* to the *vida* which precedes it accomplishes much more than simply to refresh our memory; it also serves to set the third-person *vida* into a first-person framework, thereby making explicit the first-person narrator, who, throughout the *vidas* in general, remained implicit.

Since space does not permit a complete examination of Peire's *vida*, we shall concentrate on those features which seem to have entered into the creation of *Razo Bb*. Twice the *vida* uses superlatives for Peire, once in relation to his singing ability and again with regard to his foolishness. The *vida* provides a precedent, then, for the technique of broadening, which the author of the *razo* will put to good service in his version of the story of the stolen kiss. In calling Peire *fols* and mentioning his *fulias*, the *vida* clues us in on the central motif both of the *vida* itself and of the two *razos* which grow out from it. For, the *vida* will revolve around two specific examples of the poet's foolishness, and each of the *razos* will add to these yet another case showing how Peire acted like a fool.

The verb *crezia* occurs four times in the *vida*, initially to state that Peire believed everything that he would have liked to come true, later to say that he believed he was going to conquer the empire of Constantinople, then to explain that he believed that all the ladies adored him, and, finally, to reiterate that he believed he was the most beloved of all lovers. We see now that, in inventing a comic tale around the discrepancy between what Peire believes and what the rational observer believes, the composer of our *razo* is doing nothing new. *Bb* inscribes itself into a general tradition of Peire Vidal legends which play on this fundamental opposition between "appearance" and "reality."

The *vida*'s *rics sons* "rich melodies" are transposed into *ric trobar* and *ricas fulias* in the *razo*. *Ric*, true to its meaning, is a "rich" word, which ordinarily denotes "power," "wealth," "great quantity," but which in conjunction with *trobar* becomes a technical term indicative of a highly elaborate style of versemaking.[32] The *razo* in its first use of *ric* refers to this concept familiar in Old Provençal poetics; in its second use of *ric* it transfers *ric*'s sense of complexity from an artificial to an experiential domain by associating it with Peire's *fulias* "follies" or "adventures." To link *ric* both with art (*trobar*) and experience (*fulias*) suggests that poetics and life do combine, even though the bond between them may be complicated (*ric*).

Stepping away from specific *razos* and summarizing those features common to them all, we recognize first their duplicity. They have a double frame of reference, each text being linked not only to a poem but also to a *vida* and possibly other *razos*. They characteristically work themselves out in two spaces, that of pure narration and that of their own actualization. Both *razos* examined here represent expansions in prose of particular poetic images: a synthetic lady in one, a stolen kiss in the other. The theme of recovery central to our two texts exemplifies a fundamental preoccupation of the genre as a whole, for, even as Bertran de Born and Peire Vidal are seeking through different means to win back their ladies, so too the *razo* as a literary form is seeking to recover the *intus*, or underlying thought, of the poem. Naturally, what happens inside the poet's mind is invisible but what goes into it and what emerges from it are not. The *razo* presumes to reconstruct those external experiences which, once having sunk into the poetic consciousness, later resurface as poem.

Vidas and *razos* open up poems as a way of preserving, and, indeed, celebrating the lyric universe. Paradoxically, though, they help to destroy the very thing which they work to preserve, for, by increasing the means of access to the lyric composition, they break down the integrity of the lyric world. Much that was unique to *fin' amors*—secrecy, exclusiveness, ambiguity, unattainability—gets lost when exposed and clarified in *vidas* and *razos*.

IV. *Las Razos de trobar:*
The Prose of Troubadour Poetics

A radically different view of the troubadour lyric tradition comes to us through the Catalan poet and grammarian, Raimon Vidal, author of *Las Razos de trobar* (c. 1200).[1] Whereas the biographers focus on troubadours as individuals, Vidal regards the tradition as a whole. While the composers of *vidas* and *razos* recount personal experiences which they suppose to have occasioned specific poems, the author of *Las Razos de trobar* describes *Lemosi*, the universal language of lyric poetry. The biographers, the vast majority of them anonymous, rarely call attention to themselves, or do so only through formulas such as "si com ieu vos ai dig." Vidal, however, not only identifies himself by name but keeps reminding us of his presence in the text through his frequent use of the first-person pronoun. The biographers and Vidal express themselves in prose styles which contrast conspicuously—the former, narrative; the latter, expository. Such antitheses notwithstanding, the Catalan grammarian shares with the composers of *vidas* and *razos* a unique preoccupation with the troubadours and a compelling desire to keep that poetic heritage alive.

The first eight paragraphs of *Las Razos de trobar* warrant close examination because they provide an invaluable commentary on the state of the art in a time and place at some remove from many of the best known troubadours.

> Per so qar ieu Raimon Vidals ai vist et conegut qe pauc d'omes sabon ni an saubuda la dreicha maniera de trobar, voill eu far aqest libre per far conoisser et saber qals dels trobars an mielz trobat et mielz ensenhat, ad aqelz qe·l volran aprenre, con devon segre la dreicha maniera de trobar.

"Per so qar" establishes from the very outset the tone of dogmatism which will inform the whole work. *Ieu* announces itself early, and the proper name Raimon Vidal, which stands in apposition to it, emphasizes the force of the first-person voice. The *passé composé* "ai vist et conegut" 'I have seen and known' sets up the temporal perspective for the work by suggesting a continuity between past and present. Vidal, from his vantage point in the present, is studying a phenomenon which began in the past and which has existed without interruption ever since. These two verbs *vist* and *conegut* further inform us that the grammarian bases his remarks both on personal observations (*vist*) and on what he has been able to learn (*conegut*) that is, on first- as well as second-hand knowledge. In speaking of "pauc d'omes" the author implicitly ranks himself among those 'few men' who have fathomed the true meaning of *trobar*. By combining the present and past of the verb *saber*, "sabon ni an saubuda," Raimon Vidal reveals his conviction that ignorance of the troubadour art is not a condition originating in his own day, but that misconceptions of *trobar* are as old as *trobar* itself.[2] The words "la dreicha maniera" expose Vidal's bias that there exists a single proper method for composing verses.

One of the major aspects of Vidal's task, then, will be to define this standard procedure. The repetition of the first-person pronoun, *eu*, reaffirms the central position of "I" in this enterprise. Vidal may well be writing about someone or something besides himself, but everything that is said here about Old Provençal poets and poetry reaches us only as it is conveyed by this clearly identified, strongly opinionated first-person author. The pair "far conoisser et saber" announces Raimon's distinctly pedagogical aim. His instruction will consist, on the one hand, in making known which troubadours composed the best pieces and set the best example and, on the other, in illustrating for any willing student the proper way to pursue the poet's craft. The return to the phrase "la dreicha maniera de trobar" at the end of this opening sentence suggests that these words represent the crux of Vidal's whole thought.

In the next little section Vidal protects himself against prospective critics, first by saying that if he is excessively wordy in his explanations of some matters, it is because he has observed how in many instances skills are turned into error and dispute for lack of adequate discussion. Then, having justified his wordiness, Vidal turns to the opposite fault and excuses himself for whatever omissions and oversights he may have allowed. With such apologies out of the way, the grammarian declares confidently that the intelligent reader will defend him despite any wrong things he may say or any right things he may leave unsaid. Vidal's reasoning here is elliptical. What he implies is that although his book on *trobar* can never be exhaustive, he can, by conceding its imperfection and explaining the reason behind its flaws in terms of his own shortcomings, confer upon it a certain cohesiveness. Vidal recognizes that even when there is no fault in a work, there will always be someone who can, or who thinks he can, improve upon its contents by revising or appending the original text. Judging his material adequate as it stands, Raimon Vidal issues a stern warning to posterity not to tamper with his text: "Per qu'ieu vos dig qe en neguna ren, pos basta ni ben ista, no·n deu om ren ostar ni mais metre." Vidal's concern over the corruptibility of his own work when entrusted to the public parallels another, for was it not a recognition of the corruptibility of *Lemosi* when employed by ignorant people which motivated him to write *Las Razos de trobar* in the first place?

> Totas genz cristianas, iusieuas et sarazinas, emperador, princeps, rei, duc, conte, vesconte, contor, valvasor, clergue, borgues, vilans, paucs et granz, meton totz iorns lor entendiment en trobar et en chantar, o q'en volon trobar o q'en volon entendre o q'en volon dire o q'en volon au/zir; qe greu seres en loc negun tan privat ni tant sol, pos gens i a paucas o moutas, qe ades non auias cantar un o autre o tot ensems, qe neis li pastor de la montagna lo maior sollatz qe ill aiant an de chantar. Et tuit li mal e·l ben del mont son mes en remembransa per trobadors. Et ia non trobares mot [ben] ni mal dig, po[s] trobaires l'a mes en rima, qe tot iorns [non sia] en remembranza, qar trobars et chantars son movemenz de totas galliardias.

In this second paragraph Vidal argues for the importance of his subject, *trobar*. But at the same time that he, in good rhetorical fashion, is thus wooing his prospective student, he also unwittingly provides for future generations a precious tableau of the poetic scene as it must have appeared in Catalonia at the turn of the thirteenth century.[3] Furthermore, he reveals some of his personal convictions about the nature and function of poetry, opinions which are all the more interesting because Vidal was himself a poet. *Trobar*, or the cultivation of the poetic art, acts as a binding force within society; it brings together people of all religions and all stations in life, from mighty rulers down to simple townsfolk. No longer strictly a "courtly" phenomenon, troubadour songs have become by Vidal's day a source of entertainment in places far removed from the courts where they originated. Even shepherds on the mountainside find their greatest pleasure in such songs.[4] Not only a unifying agent, *trobar* also preserves. According to Vidal, all the good and evil of the world have been immortalized by the troubadours. Finally, *trobar* has a civilizing effect on society; it inspires men to accomplish noble deeds: "... trobars et chantars son movemenz de totas galliardias." Another noteworthy aspect of Vidal's attitude as it emerges from this paragraph is that the author of *Las Razos de trobar* sets audiences on a par with poets as active participants in the poetic process: "o q·en volon trobar o q·en volon entendre o q·en volon dire o q·en volon auzir."[5]

In the third paragraph the grammarian depicts the troubadours as victims of corruption. And who are the culprits who bring down the high standards of *Lemosi* and deceive poets of good repute? Undiscerning audiences. Many of these listeners, in their fear of looking foolish, delude themselves by not admitting when they do not understand something. The wisest men, states Vidal, are those who raise questions and who wish to learn that which they do not know. Meanwhile other listeners, because of their noble upbringing, politely refrain from criticizing a bad song. But they, too, mislead the troubadours, for the noblest men, to Vidal's way of thinking, are those who praise the praiseworthy and blame that which deserves blame.

Raimon Vidal remarks (fourth paragraph) that those who think they understand something without truly understanding are incapable of learning. While recognizing, on the one hand, that there are many people whom he can never reach with his instruction, he realizes, on the other, that there is no error so great that with clear explanations from him and careful attention from them he cannot lead at least some of them from their mistakes. Thus, he contents himself with writing for the benefit of "l'una partida," that small group of people capable of profiting from his instruction. Membership into this select minority addressed by Vidal is based on two criteria. First, one must be Calatan. This fact accounts for the peculiar imbalances in the grammarian's descriptive analysis of *Lemosi*, for if Vidal seems to place undue stress on the case distinctions of nouns and adjectives, it is because Catalan does not observe any, and if he says very little about vocabulary and syntax, it is because Catalan uses most of the same words and syntactical patterns as the language of the troubadours.[6] In addition to being Catalan, however, one must also be what Vidal calls an "hom prim."

Though Raimon Vidal never stops to define exactly what he means by *prim*, he uses the term often enough and in a wide enough variety of contexts that we are able to grasp some of its subtleties. The adjective *prim* occurs twelve times in the course of this short treatise and the related adverb *primamenz* thrice.[7] Surprisingly, the *hom prim* presents himself initially as a rather annoying type. It is he who will possibly criticize Vidal for the book's inevitable imperfections; he appears, as Vidal portrays him, a smug man, a know-it-all who can always tell a person how he might have done a good job better. But the critical role of the *hom prim* has its positive aspects as well. He can be more indulgent than most readers toward the author, for the *hom prim* alone understands the complexity of the subject under discussion and the impossibility for any one person to comprehend it thoroughly. Moreover, the *hom prim*, being endowed with a quick mind, does not have to have a hundred examples set before him in order to perceive the general rule. The *hom prim* can further facilitate the grammarian's task by his willingness to tackle new material on his own. Thus, when Vidal grows weary and decides not to finish treating verbs, he appeals to the ability of the *hom prim* to execute this portion of the study on his own. Being *prim* involves a combination of instinct and training. On the one hand, Vidal cannot make an *hom prim* out of anyone who is not already inclined to be so, but, on the other, he can help to make the *hom prim* become more *prim* (*aprimar*).

> Aqest saber de trobar non fon anc/mais [mes] ni aiostatz tan ben
> en un sol luoc, mais qe cascun n'ac en son cor segon qe fon prims
> ni entendenz.

Vidal boasts that the "saber de trobar" has never before been so well put nor so well organized in any single place, except, that is, in the heart of the individual in proportion to his native excellence and intelligence. He explains that no one person has ever known all there is to know about *trobar*, for this art is too rich and subtle for any one person to comprehend in full. Not even Raimon Vidal himself has completely mastered it, as he admits quite frankly with his "eu non dic ges qe sia maistres ni parfaitz." Even so, the nature of *trobar* is such that although no one man can ever hope to know it thoroughly, the intelligent, conscientious individual may continue to refine his understanding of it. Thus, Vidal takes heart, for he sees that his book can serve as a useful guide to that man who, being endowed by nature with a "bon cor de trobar," wishes to make songs of which he need not feel ashamed.

With the sixth paragraph Vidal shifts his attention from preliminary comments about the unique character of his project to an initial attempt to define *Lemosi*:

> Totz hom qe vol trobar ni entendre deu primierament saber qe neguna parladura non es naturals ni drecha del nostre lingage, mais acella de Franza et de Lemosi et de Proenza et d'Alvergna et de Caersin. Per qe ieu vos dic qe, qant ieu parlarai de 'Lemosi', qe totas estas terras entendas et totas lor vezinas et totas cellas qe son entre ellas. Et tot l'ome qe en aqellas terras son nat ni norit an la parladura natural et drecha.

Vidal states unequivocally that *Lemosi* is the only natural and proper dialect of *trobar*. But what does he mean by *Lemosi*? *Lemosi*, as I interpret Raimon's use of it, designates two different things. First, it is the collective term used to embrace the dialects of Limousin and surrounding territories. Within this rather extensive geographical region, men are born and nourished in the natural and correct *parladura* of *Lemosi*. Thus, Vidal recognizes *Lemosi* as being first and foremost the natural vernacular which thrives untrained within a particular geographical domain. The fact that this dialect comes naturally to certain men because of where they were born does not mean, however, that these native speakers automatically use it flawlessly. When a native speaker of *Lemosi* steps over the bounds of proper usage, whether for rhyme or some other reason, the person who has acquired *Lemosi* as a foreign language is said to know it better than the person who has grown up speaking it. Vidal points out that these native speakers do not regard their linguistic liberties as faults, for, after all, they would contend, *Lemosi* is their native tongue and they should be free to use it as they wish. It is at this moment that Vidal makes a crucial distinction between *Lemosi* as the inconstant patterns of speech within a certain geographical area and a second *Lemosi*, the stable language of a highly sophisticated literature. In this second *Lemosi*, a rarefied form of the first, a standard more selective than common usage determines correctness. Because Vidal concentrates on this second kind of *Lemosi*, especially as it informed, and was informed by, troubadour verse, he sees his book as valuable, not simply to those for whom *Lemosi*, is a foreign dialect, but potentially also to those people who, by virtue of their birthplace, speak a form of it every day.

In explaining the unique virtue of *Lemosi* Vidal makes an observation which prefigures one later to be made by Dante in the *De Vulgari Eloquentia*:[8]

> La parladura francesca val mais et [es] plus avinenz a far romanz et pasturellas, mas cella de Lemosin val mais per far vers et cansons et serventes. Et per totas las terras de nostre lengage son de maior autoritat li cantar de la lenga lemosina qe de neguna autra parladura; per q'ieu vos en parlerai primeramen.

In Vidal's view "French" is better and more pleasing for *romanz* and *pasturellas*, whereas *Lemosi* is better suited for *vers*, *cansos*, and *serventes*. All of these genres are verse forms, the fundamental distinction between them being that *romanz* and *pasturellas* fall into the broad category of narrative poetry, while *cansos*, *vers*, and *serventes* come under the heading of lyric. It is significant that Vidal, who in the preceding paragraph included the dialect of "France" among those which jointly constitute *Lemosi*, now treats "French" and *Lemosi* as equal entities. He conveys through this dual classification the notion that everyone has two languages at his disposal: the one of everyday communication, which admits of variation from one geographical region to the next; the other, reserved for literary expression. In the former the dialects of *Franza* and of *Lemosi*, though identifiable as such, merge with others to form a linguistic ensemble, which bears the ambiguous name, *Lemosi*. In the latter "la parladura francesca" and "cella de Lemosin" remain distinct languages which serve divergent purposes. An author chooses a literary language, not according to where he lives, but, rather, according to what he intends to write.

> Et per totas las terras de nostre lengage son de maior autoritat li cantar de la lenga lemosina qe de neguna autra parladura; per q'ieu vos en parlerai primeramen.

A striking feature of this statement is its uniting of geography ("totas las terras") with literary performance and production ("li cantar") into a single affirmation about *Lemosi*. The term "nostre lengage" used to designate a Romance vernacular language system comprising all the various dialects of the area corresponding more or less to present-day Midi conforms to an earlier categorization; likewise, the word *parladura* used to designate any one of these dialects is consistent with terminology employed elsewhere in the book. What is new, though, is that *Lemosi*, which until now has been referred to as a *parladura* along with Catalan, Auvergnat, etc. (except for one place where it was ironically called a *lengage*), is here granted the status of *lenga*.[9] For Vidal, *Lemosi*'s status as a *lenga* is intimately connected with its participation in *li cantar*, the canon of troubadour songs. Thus the tradition of troubadour verse not only elevates *Lemosi* from an unstable dialect to a set language, it also gives it *autoritat* over the other Romance dialects. The learned ring of *autoritat* contrasts sharply with the generally plain vocabulary of Vidal's exposition and hence summons forth the formerly omnipotent Latin to which *Lemosi* is being compared. The pre-eminence of *Lemosi* among the Romance dialects could scarcely be expressed more emphatically than when Vidal contrasts *Lemosi* as a *lenga* having *autoritat* with other dialects, which he relegates to the lowly rank of "neguna autra parladura." It is no wonder, then, that after placing *Lemosi* in such an exalted position Vidal should decide to begin his discussion with it. The adverb *primeramen* 'first' suggests that Vidal will later discuss French, but in fact he never does.

The opening sentence of the following paragraph (the eighth) brings up yet another aspect of dialects--their overlap:

> Mant home son qe dizon qe *porta* ni *pan* ni *vin* non son paraolas de Lemo/sin per so car hom las ditz autresi en autras terras com en Lemosin.

Superficially, this statement does little more than inform us that three specific words--*porta*, *pan*, and *vin*--are perfectly acceptable in *Lemosi* despite the fact that they coincide with the words for 'door,' 'bread,' and 'wine' in other Romance dialects. More importantly though, this observation calls into question the effectiveness of geography as a criterion for determining where one dialect stops and another begins. By citing examples of commonplace words which span several territories, Vidal illustrates that while geography may assist in the initial, rough definition of a dialect, it cannot be treated as the ultimate standard. Now that he has demonstrated the limits of geography as a basis for deciding matters of correctness, Vidal goes on to introduce the next step in the search for the *saber de trobar*:

> Per q'ieu vos dic qe totz hom qe vuella trobar ni entendre deu aver fort privada la parladura de Lemosin. Et apres deu saber alqes de la natura de gramatica, si fort primamenz vol trobar ni ente[n]dre, car tota la parladura de Lemosin se parla naturalmenz et per cas et per [nombres et per] genres et per temps et per personas et per motz, aisi com poretz auzir aissi si ben o escoutas.

He says that whoever wishes to invent or understand troubadour verse must start with a thorough knowledge of the *parladura* of Limousin, *parladura* being the ordinary speech of the inhabitants of the area whose name the dialect bears. One must then know something about the nature of "Grammar," for *Lemosi*, like Grammar (here synonymous with Latin), operates according to case, number, and gender, as well as tense, person, and vocabulary.

The eight paragraphs just summarized provide an introduction to Raimon Vidal's work. Now begins the systematic description of the categories and flexions of *Lemosi*.[10] The prose in this central section is remarkably plain and amply supported by examples of short sentences apparently of Vidal's invention and verses of poetry from various troubadour songs. The organization of this relatively long descriptive part revolves around an unstated question: Given the mass of words and flexions which constitute *Lemosi* and the dual nature of *Lemosi* itself, how does one determine correctness? In searching for an answer, Raimon Vidal proceeds by a process of elimination.

First he shows that *gramatica* alone is not the standard. A synonym for Latin, *gramatica* differs from *Lemosi* and Romance dialects in general, primarily with regard to gender. Whereas *gramatica* has five genders-- masculine, feminine, neuter, *comuns*, and *omne--romans* 'the Romance vernacular' has only three--masculine, feminine, and *comuns*. In addition to these three genders *romans* recognizes a pseudo-neuter which manifests itself by the omission of flexional endings in certain common one-syllable words when these words are used in impersonal expressions such as *m'es car*, *mal m'es*, and *bel m'es*. Not only does *romans* deviate from *gramatica* as to the number of genders which it recognizes, but also, at least in some instances, as to the genders assigned to specific words. For example, in *gramatica* the equivalent for *arbres* is feminine and for *cors* is neuter, while in *romans* both are masculine. Meanwhile, *amor* and *mar*, which are neuter in *gramatica*, are both feminine in *romans*.

Having demonstrated that the measure for correctness is not *gramatica* alone, Vidal reveals that it is not mere *us* 'usage' either. He establishes the unreliability of *us* by showing how flexional endings are often improperly employed in everyday speech. Examples of masculine nominative singulars without -s, e.g. "le cavaliers es vengut"; "mal mi fes le caval" and plurals with -s, e.g. "vengut son los cavaliers"; "mal mi feron los cavals" prove

Vidal's point that there are abuses of language which creep into the *parladura* "per us" 'through usage.' To illustrate the complex nature of the question of correctness, Vidal cites several instances where either of two forms is acceptable. One may say either "ieu mi fas gai" or "ieu mi fas gais"; likewise one may say either "ieu mi teng per pagat" or "ieu mi teng per pagatz." In both examples the first form is grammatically correct, but the second has come to be condoned "per us de parladura."

But if ordinary usage does not serve as a valid measure of correctness, perhaps literary practice can. Thus, Vidal turns to the troubadours in order to see whether their example may be taken as authoritative. In this section Vidal cites verses from Bernart de Ventadorn, Guillem de Saint Didier, Guiraut de Borneill, Bertran de Born, and Arnaut de Mareuill to illustrate that in *Lemosi* (in contrast to other Romance dialects) nominative and vocative plurals add nothing. Sometimes, then, one finds that the troubadours exemplify proper use of *Lemosi*. Unfortunately, however, there are other times when the troubadours go astray, in particular when they allow demands of rhyme to alter the patterns endorsed by grammar and good usage. One of the most common mistakes made by the troubadours is the confusion of first- and third-person verb forms. Among those guilty of this error are Guiraut de Borneill, Peirol, Bernart de Ventadorn, Folquet de Marseille, and Peire Vidal. Obviously, then, troubadour verse, like *gramatica* and *us*, fails on its own to provide a totally reliable standard. At this point in his argument Raimon interjects a special warning to his readers to beware of "bad" poets, since it is now apparent that even the best troubadours are fallible.

Ostensibly, it is laziness that causes Raimon to conclude, prematurely it would seem, the central descriptive section of *Las Razos de trobar*. Vidal says that he cannot go into any more detail about words in the verb category "sens gran affan" 'without great effort.'[11] And why should he bother to say any more, since he has already made it clear that the small minority to whom he addresses himself does not need to have everything spelled out? "En una paraula o en duas qe ieu diga per semblan, pot entendre toz homs prims totas las autras."[12] Vidal summarizes the steps by which the *hom prim* may go beyond a knowledge of the precise points enumerated in this book to form his own judgments about *trobar*. Upon encountering words other than those mentioned in *Las Razos de trobar*, he should, first of all, use them as he hears them spoken by native speakers; next, inquire about them from those who have had formal training in *Lemosi*; and, finally, check to see how the good troubadours understood them. As if in response to our unvoiced objections that this process seems unnecessarily complicated, Vidal reminds us that "nul gran saber non po hom aver menz de gran us (et) de sotileza."

Before closing, Vidal places his discussion of *Lemosi* in a broader context. For one thing he warns against confusing certain *Lemosi* words with their "French" equivalents. But the other point which Vidal introduces right here at the end concerns one of the requirements of good composition. Heretofore Vidal has confined his comments to individual flexions and words; now, however, he speaks briefly of how words are to be joined in literary discourse. In composing, be it *cantars* 'songs' or *romans* 'romances,' one must take care lest the *razos* 'argument' be *mal continuadas* or *mal seguidas*.[13] Logic must be sustained from beginning to end if a work is to be truly whole. Vidal illustrates his point with a negative example taken from a song by Bernart de Ventadorn, *Ben m'an perdut de lai vas Ventedor*.[14] Vidal explains that in the first four stanzas Bernart claims to love his lady so much that he could never leave her but that in the fifth stanza the poet contradicts himself by saying:

> A las autras sui ueimais escazutz,
> Car una·m po, si·s vol, a son ops traire.

That Raimon Vidal should criticize Bernart's song for its *razo mal seguida* shows clearly the radical change that has occurred since the time of the troubadour and his contemporaries. The days of oxymoronic lyric moods, expressed variously as "iausen-pensiu," "mos mals aitan bos," and the like, have vanished.[15] When critics begin to demand logical consistency of a lyric poem, they shatter the sphere within which this kind of poetry operates. They are, in effect, flattening out the lyric universe, where all is possible simultaneously, and trying to make it conform to the linear scheme of the prosaic world, where only what is rational is possible and things happen one at a time in a logical sequence of causes and effects. In short, they attempt to measure poetic truth with prosaic yardsticks.

Perhaps the most distinctive feature of Vidal's book is its consolidation of poet and audience as coworkers in an endless process of language refinement. If *Lemosi* has deteriorated, the fault lies at least as much with the audience as with the poet. To entrust so great a responsibility to the listener is Vidal's way of combatting the widespread degradation of *trobar*.

The grammarian cannot prevent uneducated people from singing. The mountain shepherd will surely continue to sing as he pleases, oblivious that Raimon Vidal ever existed. Vidal can, however, educate a cultured minority so that within their own circle, restricted though it be, the purest language will be upheld.

Though Raimon Vidal announces at the beginning of his book his intention to teach "la dreicha maniera de trobar," his instructions seem to pertain more to standards of correctness in *Lemosi*, the language of troubadour verse, than to compositional technique. This apparent discrepancy between what Raimon sets out to do and what he actually accomplishes has provoked one scholar to call *Las Razos de trobar* "a disappointing work in the most literal sense of that expression"[16] and another to describe it derogatorily as a work which begins as an ingenious *ars poetica* but which ends up as a pedestrian grammar book.[17] What, then, if anything, in this text might fall within the scope of "la dreicha maniera de trobar"? For instance, does Raimon prescribe the subject matter from which the aspiring troubadour should choose? The response to this query is obviously no; indeed, not only does Raimon refrain from enumerating the subjects worthy of *Lemosi* verse, but he goes out of his way to emphasize the breadth of matters which have been immortalized by the tradition. "Tuit li mal e·l ben del mont son mes en remembransa per trobadors." And yet, Raimon does provide some model topics for the *hom prim* astute enough to discover them tucked among the expository remarks about the flexions of *Lemosi*. The sample sentences invented by the grammarian to illustrate various noun and adjective endings articulate, albeit in a very unassuming way, certain of the themes associated with the troubadour lyric tradition. Examples such as "Reis sui d'Aragon" and "ieu sui rics homs" imply nobility. "Vengut son los cavaliers" suggests knighthood. The two sentences "bo·m sap l'escut" and "ieu feric un home" connote warfare; the pair "verges es aquest homs" and "verges es aquesta femna" introduces the themes of youth and/or moral virtue. Both "ieu mi teng per pagat" and "bon m'es car m'aves onrat" summon forth the notion of recompense. "Ieu mi fas gais" and "bo·m sap le venirs" express the themes of joy and union, while "mal me fai l'anars" conveys their opposites: sorrow and separation.[18] The reader may assume that any of these topics could bear expansion into a literary composition. But does Raimon say anything about the genres appropriate for the development of the poet's chosen subject matter? The answer to this question lies in the grammarian's famous distinction between French as the language of *romanz* and *pasturellas* and *Lemosi* as the language of *vers*, *cansons*, and *serventes*.[19] In directing his attention exclusively to *Lemosi*, Raimon clearly advocates the selection of one of the three lyric genres for which this language is so eminently suited. Raimon further instructs the poet in the *dreicha maniera* by warning him not to enslave himself to form. The troubadour should never allow rhyme to take precedence over the dictates of morphology, nor should he permit the conventional formulas of courtly love to override the logical presentation of ideas.[20] Thus, Vidal, even as he is teaching his readers about the nature of *Lemosi*, is offering to the *homs prims* among them a few useful guidelines for composition—specifically, what subject matters to treat, what genres to employ, and what value to assign to the constraints of form.

Those scholars who find Vidal's book a disappointment should perhaps review the precise terms of the promises made in the prologue. Vidal never claims that he can make a good poet of just anyone, nor does he ever say that he will provide an exhaustive study of *la dreicha maniera de trobar*. The task he sets for himself is, in a sense, a larger one, for he undertakes to educate the public to the subtleties of troubadour verse by making at least some of his readers conscious of their ignorance in this domain. And here, I would argue, he succeeds.

The *Razos de trobar* is at one and the same time a singular accomplishment and an integral part of a larger thirteenth- and fourteenth-century tradition of vernacular grammars. Two books which derive directly from Raimon Vidal's grammar are the *Doctrina d'Acort* by the Italian Terramagnino da Pisa, and the *Regles de trobar* by the Aragonese Jofre de Foixà.[21]

The *Doctrina*, which dates from the end of the thirteenth century, represents an attempt to convert the *Razos de trobar* into verse. Its author, Terramagnino, eliminates many of Vidal's personal reflections, including the discussion about the interplay between poet and public. Apart from its verse form, the *Doctrina d'Acort* is innovative in its inclusion of prose paradigms and new quotations. The Italian grammarian, who postdates Raimon Vidal by more than half a century, had a knowledge of Old Provençal which was, in Marshall's words, "uncertain and fragmentary." Terramagnino probably gleaned all that he knew of the language from the combined study of *Las Razos de trobar* and those few troubadour poems to which he had access.[22]

While the *Doctrina* tried to put *Las Razos de trobar* into poetry, another late thirteenth-century grammar, the *Regles de trobar*, sought to rework *Las Razos* in a different way. Jofre de Foixà wished to provide an exposition of "lo saber de trobar" which would be comprehensible to a public unacquainted with Latin. Because he assumes no prior knowledge of grammar on the part of his reader, Jofre avoids Latinate terminology and explains at length the most elementary points of syntax and versification. Although Jofre borrows heavily from his predecessor Raimon Vidal, he demonstrates a critical spirit and open-mindedness which are uniquely his. He rejects Vidal's dogmatic views on certain verb inflections and admits on numerous occasions the possibility distasteful to his rigid forebear that variant forms might be equally correct. Jofre de Foixà is the first vernacular grammarian to treat the definite article as a linguistic feature in its own right. Jofre's attitude differs markedly from Raimon Vidal's. While Vidal sees *Lemosi* as a vital language and can turn both to native speakers of his own day and to troubadours of the past to verify how its rules have been used and abused, Jofre de Foixà considers *Lemosi* a dead language and, therefore, regards the troubadours, through whose poetry the language is preserved, as final authorities in questions of correctness.[23]

These three grammars, *Las Razos*, *La Doctrina*, and *Las Regles*, are all firmly rooted in the lyric tradition. The language which they promote is one of ideal literary usage as it can be reconstructed primarily (though, in the case of *Las Razos de trobar*, not exclusively) from *li cantar*, the extant corpus of troubadour songs. Examples drawn from well-known poems give substance to their analyses. They are practical manuals which address themselves to a public interested in *Lemosi* on account of its poetry.

Quite different from the aforementioned grammars, the *Donatz Proensals* of Uc Faidit (1240), sets literary practice aside in its attempt to fit the vernacular of the Midi into the conventional framework of Latin grammar. The title *Donatz*, which by the Middle Ages had become a synonym for "primer," may be apocryphal, but, whether authentic or not, this title aptly conveys the author's desire to systematize Old Provençal in the same way that the fifth-century grammarian Donatus systematized Latin in his *Ars minor*.[24] Faidit's general faithfulness to the paradigms of Latin leads him to omit the article, the comparison of adjectives, and the compound perfect of verbs; however, his adherence to the Latin model is not blind. In discussing the neuter, for instance, Uc Faidit sees that Old Provençal diverges from Latin. He admits that in his language "neuters" behave like masculines, but he does not go so far as to suggest that Old

Provençal may not have a neuter. Uc Faidit often permits multiple forms, since his chief objective, in sharp contrast to the "dreicha maniera" aim of Raimon Vidal, is inclusiveness.[25]

Uc Faidit points toward a new kind of grammar. He tries to set Old Provençal into a scheme broad enough to encompass every case, even conflicting ones, which non-literary, as well as literary, practice might afford. Uc's system of language, then, has literature as a subset, whereas Raimon Vidal's system is itself a subset of literature. The diminishing dependence of linguistic analysis on literature prepares the way for speculative grammar, where the standard of correctness in language is not literary precedent, but logic.

One should not cut off a discussion of the Old Provençal grammatical tradition without looking ahead to the middle of the fourteenth century, where we find the *summum opus* of Old Provençal grammar, rhetoric, poetics, and metrics. This three-volume work called the *Leys d'Amors* is a veritable encyclopedia of poetic composition, covering everything about troubadour poetry, from its underlying philosophical tenets about the power of God and the nature of love to its external features such as pronunciation, versification, rhetorical figures, and morphology.[26]

Meanwhile, alongside *Las Razos* and its imitations stands a very different kind of grammar book produced in the Middle Ages. In the second half of the twelfth century at the University of Paris, Peter Helias wrote a commentary on Priscian which revolutionized grammatical studies. Caught up in the enthusiasm for the rediscovery of Aristotle, Peter sought to establish an explicitly philosophical basis for Priscian's descriptive rules. Grammar, which had been the handmaiden of literature ever since the Greek grammarians of the first century B.C., came back under the sway of philosophy.[27] Speculative grammar could not and did not, however, fully replace the *ars grammatica*.

A modern student of medieval rhetoric James J. Murphy has remarked that "what seems to have happened is that the monolithic *ars grammatica* of Donatus and Priscian . . . simply broke up into its constituent parts around the year 1200."[28] Thus, at the same moment that the lyric was undergoing a process of fragmentation which resulted in *vidas*, *razos*, and grammar books, grammar, too, was splitting generically into separate areas of inquiry: traditional study of syntax and phonology (e.g.

Las Razos de trobar), ars ritmica, and *grammatica speculativa. Las Razos de trobar* is situated, then, at a critical point in the redefinition of two distinct traditions, the *ars grammatica* and the troubadour lyric.

V. The Poetics of Copying: The Scribe as Artist in the *Chansonniers* and Dante's *Vita Nuova*

In looking back on the troubadours from the perspective of the *vidas*, *razos*, and grammars, we have seen the twelfth-century lyric in a certain very important light. Our image of the tradition is not complete, however, until we have also looked beyond the individual genres of *canso*, *vida*, *razo*, and grammatical manual, toward a reintegrated and durable whole. This resolution is effected in the "book." And it is the scribes, who, with their eyes fixed on the future, gathered up the work of the past into the great *chansonniers* of the thirteenth and fourteenth centuries.

Although many Old Provençal *chansonniers* are purely anthologies of poems, some of them contain *vidas* and *razos* as well. In all, there are twenty biography-bearing manuscripts, which range in date from the thirteenth to the eighteenth centuries.[1] No two manuscripts record exactly the same set of biographical texts, the discrepancies being, in some cases, minimal, as between *I* and *K*, where eighty-five of the eight-six *vidas* preserved by each are identical, in others, extreme, as between *F*, whose only biographical pieces are a set of *razos* for Bertran de Born, and *P*, whose broad range of biographical matter curiously does not include any *razos* for Bertran.[2] The choice and arrangement of entries in the *chansonniers* reflect the varying extents to which the compilers of such songbooks believed that prose pieces could be integrated into a context of verse. A quick comparison of two of the major songbooks of Old Provençal poems will help to clarify how this process of compilation works.

The first of the two *chansonniers* to be considered here, known as *I* and presently located in Paris at the Bibliothèque Nationale, is apparently the work of an Italian scribe of the thirteenth century.[3] The organizing principle of *Chansonnier I* is twofold: the songs it records are classified both according to genre and, within each genre, according to poet. The book comprises three parts of unequal size; the first and longest (folios 11*r* to 150*r*) contains *cansos* and 67 *vidas*. The general pattern in Part I is this: a brightly colored miniature, the name of the poet and a *vida* (all in red letters) precede the set of *cansos* attributed to each troubadour. Part II, a collection of *tensos*, presents miniatures and *vidas* for five poets. Part III, an anthology of *sirventes*, provides prose accounts--a mixture of *vidas* and *razos*--for fourteen poets. The cohesiveness of *I* is a function of several factors. First, its uniform handwriting indicates that *I* is a single project executed by a particular clerk. Second, the presence of a table of contents bespeaks a deliberate plan on the part of the copyist. Third, the absence of any appended material suggests that both the original scribe and those who succeeded him considered this a completed work and saw fit to respect its integrity.

Having established that *I* does have a definite plan, one may inquire as to how this organization might reflect a specific attitude toward the *vidas* and *razos*. Perhaps the most remarkable feature of the *vidas* in *I* is their quantity. Although there is not a biography for every troubadour whose poems are preserved in *I*, the inclusion of *vidas* for eighty-five poets nonetheless constitutes an impressive representation. There is no discernible connection between the fame of the poet and the length of the *vida* devoted to him; the *vida* for Guillem de Peiteus, for example, is meager, while that for Guillem de la Tor is ample.[4] Nor does there appear to be any relation between the number of poems recorded for a given troubadour and the completeness of the *vida* about him. Lanfranc Cigala's eighteen *cansos* are preceded by a life summary consisting of a few short sentences, whereas Savaric de Malleo's lone *tenso* is introduced by a comparatively intricate *vida*.[5] Chronology apparently has little or nothing to do with how much the biography tells us about a given poet. Several of the *vidas* for early troubadours (e.g. Jaufré Rudel) are fairly informative; meanwhile *vidas* for some of the later poets (e.g. Albert Marques) are often quite sketchy.[6] Nor does the fact that a troubadour has a biography at all give us any indication of the extent of his reputation, for Marcabru and Raimbaut d'Aurenga are among the most notable poets in the tradition, and there are no biographical entries for either of them, while such obscure troubadours as Bertran del Pojet and Elias Fonsalada each have a *vida* devoted to them.[7] The *I*-scribe seems more concerned with assembling a set as complete as possible of troubadour lives and songs than with making critical evaluations through a deliberate exclusion or amplification of any existing *vida* material. Hence, on two occasions when he apparently had no *vida* at hand (Raimbaut d'Aurenga and Bonifaci Calvo), he reserved space, as though he meant to record one there later.[8]

It is not, however, merely the number of biographies in *I* that merits notice; of prime interest also is the way in which they are incorporated into the *chansonnier*. Each *vida*, situated as it is, immediately ahead of the set of texts attributed to the poet whom it portrays, manifests the scribe's belief that these prose texts are tightly bound to poetry. In *I*, then, *vidas* serve as little prefaces; they have no real existence of their own, as witnessed both by the fact that they are individually grafted onto bodies of poems and by the fact that they are not mentioned in the table of contents.

The occurrence of *razos* in *I* is very revealing. To be sure, there are comparatively few of them, eighteen in all, seventeen of which pertain to a single troubadour, Bertran de Born;[9] nevertheless, the inclusion of any *razos* at all in this early manuscript with its wealth of *vidas* argues persuasively for the contemporaneity of these two prose genres. This is not to deny that the majority of *razos* may have been composed much later, but, rather, to affirm that the tradition of *razos*, even if still young, did already exist in the thirteenth century when *Chansonnier I* was compiled. Each of the nineteen *razos* in *I* is placed right before the specific poem which it explains and thus, like the *vida*, functions primarily as a preface. It is curious that the *razos* occur uniquely in part III, that is, in the collection of *sirventes*. Subsequent manuscripts will, of course, include *razos* commenting on *cansos* and *tensos* in addition to *sirventes*, but the fact that *I* and *K* offer *razos* for *sirventes* only and that the other two thirteenth-century manuscripts, *A* and *B*,[10] provide no *razos* at all would seem to indicate that the politically oriented *sirventes*, earlier shown to be singularly well-suited to adaptation as a *razo*, may, indeed, have been the parent of this prose genre.

The specific intent of *I*, if indeed there is one other than to be as all-inclusive as possible, is political. The prominence of the insurrectionist Bertran de Born helps to account for the political bias of the *chansonnier*.[11] Moreover, the memorable *vidas* for Savaric de Malleo, the Dalfi d'Alvergne, Peire Cardenal, Folquet de Marseilla, and Raimon de Miraval must surely have aroused the loyalties of expatriated members of that élite society which had fostered the troubadours for a century or more.[12]

A second great *chansonnier*, *P*, currently located at the Biblioteca Laurenziana in Florence, begins in a handwriting of the fourteenth century and concludes with a date: March 28, 1310.[13] But what happens between the beginning and the end is not so simple as one might think. Evidently some of the original folios were lost and later replaced by the final pages of a fifteenth-century manuscript. These inserted folios (39 - 54) are precisely those containing the *vidas* and *razos*; thus it would appear that the biographies of *P*, despite their medial position in a fourteenth-century *chansonnier*, actually belong to a subsequent time. Since, however, our concern here is not with authenticity in a rigorously historical sense, we can, rather, value the biographies of *P* for what they represent, literally speaking-i.e. an autonomous set of prose narratives, collected originally as the concluding section of one manuscript, but detachable enough to be lifted from there and slipped into the middle of an earlier, unrelated *chansonnier*.

Unlike *I*, which never dissociates the individual *vida* or *razo* from the poem it introduces, *P* segregates the prose texts from the troubadour verses. *P* is further characterized by its unusually high proportion of *razos*, twenty as opposed to its thirteen *vidas*. The consolidation of biographical texts into independent blocks and the predominance of *razos* over *vidas* point toward new developments in vernacular prose.

The method by which the compiler of *P*'s biographies binds off *razos* reflects his unique understanding of how one prose piece may lead into another. Whereas *razos* in other manuscripts often end either by citing the first line of the poem being explained or by recording the poem in its entirety, *P* characteristically gives the whole of the particular stanza upon which the *razo* is based. The effect of *P*'s technique of quoting is that the *razo*, no longer a mere gloss or preface to a poem, appears, instead, as a self-contained narrative unit, subsuming relevant passages of poetry into a framework of narrative prose.

Whether there is unity of content in the *P*-biographies is debatable. Guido Favati, in his critical essay *Biografie di trovatori* (Genoa, 1970), argues that there is.[14] According to him, *P* has a definite character, derived largely from the editor's predilection for stories on the theme of a lost love regained. Certainly there is a striking number of incidents in which a suitor wins back his lady. Gaucelm Faidit, at fault for having believed malicious gossip about Jordana d'Ebreun, prevails upon her to pardon him by telling her that he is about to leave on a crusade and by pointing out aphoristically that those who forgive readily are readily forgiven. In another account Raimbaut de Vaqueiras is restored to favor with his Beatritz through the efforts of this lady's dull-witted brother, who naïvely encourages the moping poet to join in the merriment at his court. Elsewhere, Richart de Berbezill wins back his beloved "Mielz-de-Dompna" by enlisting a hundred knights and their ladies to fall down on their knees in front of her. Similarly, Pons de Capdoill regains his love by arranging for three highly respected ladies to plead his case for him. And Uc de Saint Circ, having abandoned a certain Lady Clara on the basis of false reports about her infidelity, repents of his folly and engages one of Clara's close friends to do what she can to procure a reconciliation for him. Favati's argument for a unifying theme in *P* is further bolstered by this manuscript's exceptional presentation of the famous Guillem de Cabestaing story. The major development of this tale is the same in *P* as in all the other manuscripts which include it. The jealous husband slays the wife's lover and serves his cooked heart to the unsuspecting wife. When the husband informs her of what she has consumed, she declares it to be the best thing that she has ever eaten; whereupon, she throws herself from her balcony to a heroic death. *P*, however, introduces a character and a subplot which occur in no other version. This new character is Agnes, the Count of Castel-Rossillon's sister-in-law, and the incident linking her to the rest of the narrative involves a confusion costing Guillem the temporary loss of his lady Margarida's love. The Count of Castel-Rossillon, seeing the smitten look in Guillem's eye, asks him if he is in love; the poet, unable to lie, says yes, and, when questioned about the object of his affection, declares it to be Agnes. Agnes, knowing what a precarious position Guillem is in and noticing the pained expression on the poet's face, pretends to reciprocate his professed love for her. The Count goes back and reports to his wife that the troubadour is having an affair with her sister. Margarida is furious and determines never to see Guillem again. But if it was Agnes who, acting with every good intention, caused the rift between the lovers, it is also she who patches things up, for she personally reassures her sister that the profession of love between her and Guillem was all a hoax.[15]

Perhaps even the *vida* for Gausbert de Poicibot could be considered a story about the recovery of love. To classify it as such seems somewhat arbitrary, however, for the events in Gausbert's life have nothing to do with erring lovers and lost loves, at least not in the ordinary sense. Gausbert errs geographically only, while the sense in which his wife is lost is strictly moral. The *vida* does not recount how a poet wins back a lady for himself and his own pleasure, but, rather, how he restores her lost soul to God by removing her from a life of debauchery and leading her to a monastery. The tone of this text is solemn, in sharp contrast to the characteristic levity of other stories on the general theme of a "lost love regained." The clerk, possibly in reaction to the sobriety of Gausbert's *vida*, juxtaposes Gausbert de Poicibot with the Monk of Montaudon, the former taking us from the secular world into the monastery and the latter, successfully, bringing us out of the monastery and back into the secular world.[16]

Although Favati is correct in emphasizing the frequency of the motif of recovery in the biographies of many of the poets portrayed in *P*, this theme is by no means universal. Consider, for example, Raimon de Miraval, who lost without ever retrieving both wife and mistress; Gui d'Uisel, who lost irrevocably his lady to another man by refusing to marry her; and Aimeric de Peguillan, who, as just retribution for having beaten a man over the head, lost permanently his right to dwell in his native Toulouse.[17] Thus, *P*, though marked by a penchant for a particular theme, does not confine itself to this one subject.

But how do the grammatical treatises fit into the *chansonnier* scheme? *Las Razos de trobar* appears in five manuscripts. In two of these, Raimon Vidal's work is accompanied simply by more grammatical treatises; in the other two, however, it is set in a context consisting not just of grammars but of biographies and poems as well.[18] *P*, for example, contains an anthology of troubadour poems, an assortment of *vidas* and *razos*, a collection of *coblas*, Uc Faidit's *Donatz proensals*, an anonymous Provençal-Italian glossary, and Raimon Vidal's *Razos de trobar*. At the end of the *Razos de trobar* the scribe signs his name: "Petrus Bezzoli de Eugebio fecit hoc opus." One might be tempted to say that this "opus" stands as a perfect fusion of all three generic types which we have been discussing. However, as we know already, *Chansonnier P* is not quite so deliberately structured as it might, at first glance, appear. The *vidas* and *razos*, though they are found between the lyric poems and the grammers, are manifestly the work of a later scribe. Furthermore, two other copyists appended unrelated Old French texts to the work signed by Petrus.[19] All things considered, true coalescence of *vidas, razos,* and grammars within an Old Provençal *chansonnier* probably does not come about until the fifteenth century. And even at that, the kind of synthesis of material produced within a *chansonnier* is strictly mechanical, a large-scale cut-and-paste job. It took a Dante to see the literary possibilities implicit in the structure of the *chansonnier* and to exploit them consciously in a work of his own. Such, I would submit, is his intent in the *Vita Nuova*.[20]

Whereas the *chansonniers*, and this would include signed ones like *P*, may not properly be treated as literature, Dante's *Vita Nuova* cannot be viewed otherwise. Although the Romance vernacular tradition is replete with self-conscious literary compostions that stand in opposition to the mechanically compiled *chansonniers*, none seems quite so germane to our present inquiry as the *Vita Nuova*. Its peculiar appropriateness inheres to a great extent in its format, which expressly emulates that of such manuscripts as we have been examining. At the outset of the *Vita Nuova* Dante ironically relinquishes his authorial power by assuming the passive role of a copyist engaged in the humble task of transcribing entries from the inclusive book of his memory into a smaller book devoted exclusively to that portion of his memory pertaining to his "new life". The Book of Memory functions not merely as an introductory device but also as the central metaphor around which the whole work is organized.[21]

In terms of form, the most conspicuous feature of the *Vita Nuova* is its mixture of poetry and prose. Now, this same thing could be said of the *chansonniers*, but in them one dare not go much further than that in looking for structural patterns. In the *Vita Nuova*, however, the separation into poetry and prose is only a preliminary step toward discerning subtler designs, which impart harmonious complexity to the carefully planned literary entity which we know as Dante's little book. The *Vita Nuova* maybe broken down into three movements, which are defined not only by the nature of the events that they relate but also by the kind and distribution of poems that they contain.[22]

Let us consider first the organization of the poems. There is an admirable regularity in the arrangement of the work's thirty-one songs. The first movement (chaps. 1-16) has nine sonnets and one non-sonnet; the second movement (chaps. 17-31) has a *canzone*, four non-*canzoni*, another *canzone*, four more non-*canzoni*, and a third *canzone*; and the final movement (chaps. 32-42), like the initial section, has nine sonnets and one non-sonnet. The poems of the *Vita Nuova* as a whole revolve around those of its middle section. It is no mere coincidence that the central *canzone* of the central movement presents a poetic prefiguration of the death of Beatrice. This song's position at dead center of all the poems in the *Vita Nuova* (there are fifteen ahead of it and fifteen after it) reflects structurally Dante's understanding of Love's enigmatic revelation of himself (chap. 12): "ego tantum centrum circuli, cui simili modo se habent circumferentiae partes."²³ Beatrice's death, like love itself, marks the center of a circle, the circle in this case being the poet's experience, for this cardinal event informs the poet's view of everything that went before it as well as all that came after it. This description of the *Vita Nuova*'s intricate symmetry, though sketchy to be sure, illustrates the purposefulness with which the poems were selected and arranged.

The prose passages, too, work according to a plan. They constitute a continuous story about Dante's ever-deepening love for Beatrice. That there are admitted digressions, such as chapter ten, which tells of the effect of the lady's greeting, argues convincingly for the existence of a well-defined narrative line with respect to which something may be judged relevant or irrelevant. Take, for instance, the discussion of the number nine, which Dante sees as pertinent to his main theme, or recall, to the contrary, the three-point explanation of why a detailed report on the death of Beatrice would not be in keeping with the narrative content as Dante has conceived it.²⁴

The prose accounts found in the *Vita Nuova* belong to two types--*ragioni* and *divisioni*.²⁵ Etymologically and substantially, the *ragioni* are akin to *razos*. It is a known fact that Dante was familiar with some of the Old Provençal *chansonniers*; thus, we can be sure that it was with full consciousness of the vernacular prose tradition of *vidas* and *razos* that Dante chose to entitle his poetic autobiography a *vita* and to call the narrative parts within it *ragioni*.²⁶ The *ragione*, in imitation of its archetype, functions in a close relationship both to a poem and to other prose passages. With respect to poems, Dante's *ragioni* explain the circumstances surrounding the invention of a specific song or group of songs, while with respect to other *ragioni*, they contribute to the advancement of the single narrative line, whose oneness makes of the *Vita Nuova* a true book as opposed to a *chansonnier*-style anthology.

The second kind of prose, the *divisioni*, has no parallel in the *chansonniers*. These are analytical passages that divide the poems into parts. Though not themselves narrative, they break down poems according to essentially narrative criteria. The purpose of the *divisioni* is expressly stated on several occasions. In chap. 14, for example, we read that "la divisione non si fa se non per aprire la sentenzia de la cosa divisa"; or again in chap. 19 Dante explains: "Questa canzone, acciò che sia meglio intesa, la dividerò più artificiosamente che l'altre cose di sopre."[27] The divisions serve, then, to open up the meaning of a poem on the assumption that the accessibility of a poetic composition is directly proportional to the number of times one divides it. That is to say, the more divisions made, the clearer the poem.

Throughout the first thirty chapters *divisioni* follow the poems which they treat. In chap. 31, however, the pattern inverts. Just before recording the third *canzone*, Dante explains: "e acciò che questa canzone paia rimanere più vedova dopo lo suo fine, la dividerò prima che io la scriva."[28] From this point on, divisions precede their poems. The moment at which this switch takes place coincides, not by accident, with a turning point in the poet's experience. Beatrice's death has become an event, not only in the imagination of the poet but also in reality. Therefore, it is fitting that henceforth the poem, a verbal projection of Dante's feelings, should be left alone, widowed.

Intimately involved with the structure of any piece of discourse is its voice. And if the structure of the *Vita Nuova* with its various forms of poetry and prose woven into tight geometric patterns is complex to say the least, so too the voice which is able to articulate them all. Both the *chansonnier* and the *Vita Nuova* build around three distinct points of view, each of which determines a particular space. Think first of the *chansonnier*. Here the most exclusive region is established by the first-person present of the lyric poems. A second space is defined by the third-person past of narration as it is found in the *vidas* and *razos*. In this second domain there is, ostensibly, no voice; narrative events appear to unfold without human intervention. These events grow out of, and graft themselves onto, lyric poems, hence operate in a space which includes the primordial realm of the lyric universe. A third space is created by the first-person present of the *razos*. As a general rule this voice expresses itself formulaically in phrases such as "si cum ieu vos ai dig." This final domain is the most comprehensive of all, for its "I," be he *jongleur* or scribe, controls which songs and which narratives are to occupy a position within his space.

The *Vita Nuova*, likewise, comprises three concentric spaces analogous, though not identical, to those of the typical *chansonnier*. At the center is the closed lyric world, articulated by the first-person voice of Dante the poet.

Radiating outward from there is the realm of the *ragioni*. Like *razos*, *ragioni* are set in the past; unlike *razos*, they reflect the outlook of a first-person figure, Dante the poet-turned-autobiographer. In accordance with the *chansonnier*-model, the *Vita Nuova* contains a third "I," who makes himself known in the present-tense, expository prose: this "I" might be described as Dante the poet-autobiographer-turned-scribe. As compiler and transcriber of the book, this third "I" makes the *divisioni*, determines the material to be recorded, articulates the effect of Beatrice's greeting, explains the significance of the number nine, and discusses the licenses and limitations of poetry versus prose.

Although this threefold analysis accounts nicely for all the voices in the *chansonniers*, it does not suffice in the *Vita Nuova*, since behind the scribe of the little book lurks a silent but omnipotent author. And it is this author, Dante, who has the final say in shaping the work. All the different voices share a common source in him; hence, through whatever lips Dante may elect to speak, the whole of the *Vita Nuova* remains his alone. A disturbing paradox arises, however, in the assumption of the scribal guise, for, in presuming to be a scribe, Dante denies the same authorial power which his willful choice of the role affirms.

The dialectic between Dante the omniscient author and Dante the obedient scribe is one of the main contributors to the *Vita Nuova*'s "literariness." By splitting himself, Dante opens up his poetic consciousness in much the same way that he lays bare the sense of poems by breaking them down into *divisioni*. As author-turned-scribe, he calls attention to the multiple steps in the formation of his book and brings to the fore the compiler, who throughout the *chansonnier* tradition had confined himself to working anonymously behind the scenes. In light of our preoccupations in this essay, the genius of the *Vita Nuova* might well lie in that it transforms into an overt literary operation the process of compilation which had been functioning inconspicuously in *chansonniers* for more than a century.

Just as with our discussion of the *consonniers*, our comments on the *Vita Nuova* lead us eventually to ask: But how does the notion of grammar fit into Dante's scheme? First, the *divisioni*, by breaking the poems down into parts, give information which, according to the comprehensive perspective of the *ars grammatica*, would be considered grammatical in nature. Moreover, the process of construction informing the whole of the *Vita Nuova*, whereby the implicit workings of a *chansonnier* are rendered explicit, could be viewed as "grammaticalization" in the broadest meaning of that term. However, for a treatment of language *per se*, or "grammar" in a narrower sense, we must look beyond a literary composition like the *Vita Nuova*. It is at this point that, for our purposes, the *De Vulgari Eloquentia* enters the picture.[29] That Dante should set aside, as he did in this work, a special place to examine the nature of language within the format of a Latin *tractatus* is not surprising if we consider that this work postdates that of the earlier speculative grammarians, who had begun to consider the study of language a separate branch of knowledge quite independent of--indeed opposed to--the discourse of literature. What is remarkable, though, is that, despite the philosophical orientation of his inquiry, Dante arrives at an understanding of language whose "grammar" is based, not on speculation, but on the ideal usage inherent in its own cultural heritage.

Dante, writing a full century after Raimon Vidal, echoes, probably wittingly, many of the ideas expressed by his predecessor. Both men define dialects geographically.[30] Both recognize that there is a certain amount of lexical overlap among related dialects. Vidal mentions 'door,' 'bread,' and 'wine'; Dante cites 'love,' 'God,' 'heaven,' 'sea,' 'earth,' 'is,' 'lives,' 'dies,' 'loves.'[31] Both see the numerous Romance dialects as belonging to the same family. Vidal refers to them jointly as *Lemosi* or "nostre lingage"; meanwhile, Dante goes a step further by explaining not only that the three dialects—*oc, oïl,* and *sì*—belong to a single language group but also that they originate from a common source.[32] Furthermore, both grammarians realize that language changes over space and over time. Although Raimon Vidal never actually states this fact, his recognition of the two-dimensional flexibility of language is implicit in the *dreicha maniera*, whereby men may counteract linguistic change by turning back in space to the example set by native speakers and in time to the example set by the troubadours of a former day. But if Vidal merely hints at the synchronic and diachronic aspects of variation in language, Dante examines them closely.[33]

In accordance with its more philosophical approach, the *De Vulgari Eloquentia* investigates certain notions which *Las Razos de trobar* does not question. For instance, Vidal takes for granted the meaning of *gramatica*. Perhaps he believes that his reader already knows what it is, or maybe he assumes that his particular interpretation of the concept will be clear enough from the contexts in which he uses it. *Gramatica* occurs twice in *Las Razos de trobar*, once with reference to Donatus' eight parts of speech and once in distinction to *romans* 'the Romance dialects.' Dante, on the other hand, defines *gramatica* expressly in the opening chapter of the treatise, as the secondary, artificial language passed down from Classical antiquity and learned only through assiduous study.[34] Furthermore, whereas Raimon Vidal merely accepts the fact of diversification into dialects, Dante explores the causes behind linguistic pluralism, tracing it all the way back to its first source, in the Tower of Babel.[35] Another distinction is that while Vidal does not challenge the assumption that lyric poetry is the worthiest form of literary expression, Dante proves it so, establishing first that poetry is superior to prose and then that the *canzone* is superior to other kinds of poetry.[36] Similarly, whereas Raimon Vidal takes it as a foregone conclusion that *Lemosi*, as the language of *li cantar*, is preeminent among Romance dialects, Dante goes to great lengths to determine which vernacular speech is the most illustrious; in his quest he considers one by one the various local dialects of Italy, only to opt in the end for none of them.[37]

Both Vidal and Dante believe in a pre-existent standard of correctness, which, when properly applied, can transform ordinary vernacular speech into a worthy instrument for literature. For Vidal, this standard resides in *li cantar*, i.e. the body of troubadour songs; it is not to be identified with any particular poet. Dante's standard is analogous to Vidal's in that it inheres in the collectivity of Italian dialects, without, however, being identical to any one of them. It is, indeed, like a panther, sending forth its perfume everywhere, yet being visible nowhere.[38] One might do well to clarify at this point that while neither Vidal nor Dante invents the standard which he so proudly promotes, Dante has to work much harder than his predecessor to make his standard known. *Lemosi*, as a literary language, is already a familiar term by the time that Vidal undertakes *Las Razos de trobar*. The troubadours themselves often used the name *Lemosi* to designate the language of their verse.[39] The *vulgare illustre*, on the contrary, has received no such recognition. Dante's task, then, is to prove that this standard, which he is the first to examine, has, like the *lenga lemosina*, long been operative.

Las Razos de trobar and the *De Vulgari Eloquentia*, though treating a common subject, i.e. the discovery of a standard literary language derived, at least in part, from vernacular speech, differ in their intents. Vidal writes for the unique benefit of the *hom prim*; his book is a practical manual, setting forth in a more or less systematic fashion various features of *Lemosi*. Its primary purpose is to perpetuate a certain poetic heritage. Dante, however, claims to address no one in particular. The *De Vulgari Eloquentia* is a more theoretical essay, probing the very nature of language and poetic form. Its chief goal is not so much to preserve the past as to prepare the way for the future, when Italian will surpass both French and Provençal as a literary language.

A hundred years have witnessed a significant expansion in the scope of Romance literature. Vidal divides vernacular literature into *romans* and *pasturellas* on the one hand and *cansos*, *vers* and *sirventes* on the other.[40] The distinction between these two sets of genres lies in the fact that *romans* and *pasturellas* are narrative, while *cansos, vers,* and *sirventes* are lyric. All, however, are poetry. By the early fourteenth century, though, when Dante surveys vernacular literature, poetry is no longer the unrivaled mode of literary expression. Dante declares that the *lingua oïl* is best suited for compositions in prose and *oc* for those in verse. In addition to the inclusion of prose as a legitimate form of literature, Dante further opens the embrace of vernacular literary culture by signaling the twofold preeminence of Italian (*sì*), as the medium of the subtlest and sweetest verse and as the vernacular closest to Latin.[41]

Thus, the *De Vulgari Eloquentia* accomplishes for vernacular speech the same thing that the *Vita Nuova* achieves for vernacular poetics. In both of these early endeavors Dante makes manifest a preexistent vernacular culture, which, in the case of the *Vita Nuova*, can be traced back to the Old Provençal *chansonniers* and similarly constructed "books" and which, in the case of the *De Vulgari Eloquentia*, has its roots in the troubadours' self-conscious use of vernacular language as an effective medium for poetry of the highest order.

NOTES

Chapter I

[1] Alfred Jeanroy, *La Poésie lyrique des troubadours*, 2 vols. (Toulouse and Paris: Privat and Didier, 1934), 2:69. For a medieval definition of the *canso*, see the anonymous treatise known as *De doctrina de compondre dictats*, edited by J. H. Marshall, in *The "Razos de trobar" of Raimon Vidal and Associated Texts* (London: Oxford University Press, 1972), pp. 95, 97.

[2] Moshé Lazar, *Amour courtois et fin' amors dans la littérature du XIIe siècle* (Paris: Klincksieck, 1964), pp. 55-85.

[3] It is because of this preoccupation on the part of individual troubadours with the limits of the *canso* that I have described it as a "rather narrowly defined genre." Different poets, however, sometimes had different ideas about what those limits were. Thus, it is difficult to assign one specific definition applicable to all *cansos* by all troubadours, even though each troubadour seems to have had a more or less set notion of what a *canso* was. Paul Zumthor ("Classes and Genres in Medieval Literature," in *A Medieval French Miscellany: Papers of the 1970 Kansas Conference on Medieval Literature*, ed. Norris J. Lacy [Lawrence: University of Kansas Press, 1972], p. 27), while generally believing that medieval authors did not think of poetic texts as organized into genres, makes an exception for the *canso*, which, he concedes, was, for a brief time at least, identified as a precise genre.

[4] Lazar, ed., *Bernard de Ventadour, troubadour du XIIe siècle: Chansons d'amour* (Paris: Klincksieck, 1966), p. 148; *De doctrina*, pp. 95, 97; Marshall, "*Le Vers* au XIIe siècle: genre poétique?", in *Actes et mémoires du IIIe Congrès international de langue et littérature du Midi de la France, Bordeaux 1961* (Bordeaux, 1965), 55-63.

[5] Antoine Thomas, ed., *Poésies complètes de Bertran de Born* (Toulouse: Privat, 1888), p. 95.

[6] *De doctrina*, pp. 95-96, 97; Suzanne Thiolier-Mejean, *Les Poésies satiriques et morales des troubadours du XIIe siècle à la fin du XIIIe siècle* (Paris: Nizet, 1978), pp. 28-34.

[7] *De doctrina*, pp. 97, 98; Marshall, "The Isostrophic *descort* in the Poetry of the Troubadours," *Romance Philology* 35 (1981): 130-57.

[8] Joseph Linskill, ed., *The Poems of the Troubadour Raimbaut de Vaqueiras* (The Hague: Mouton, 1964), pp. 191-98.

[9] Walter T. Pattison, ed., *The Life and Works of the Troubadour Raimbaut d'Orange* (Minneapolis: University of Minnesota Press, 1952), p. 152.

[10] L. T. Topsfield, *Troubadours and Love* (Cambridge: Cambridge University Press, 1975), pp. 14-15, 152; Hans-Robert Jauss ("Littérature médiévale et théorie des genres," *Poétique* 1 [1970]: 83) argues that the *gap* never succeeded in becoming an autonomous literary genre.

[11] As Topsfield (*Troubadours*, p. 153) remarks: "Raimbaut ... is mocking the nicely formulated genres of the literary pundits, and at the same time the vapourings of precious poets covering their inadequacy with new names for old genres." See also Pattison, p. 154, n. 1; and p. 42.

[12] Hendrik van der Werf, *The Chansons of the Troubadours and Trouvères: A Study of the Melodies and their Relation to the Poems* (Utrecht: A. Oosthoek's Uitgeversmaatschappij NV, 1972), p. 63. Van der Werf argues that the melody, though certainly a necessary component of the *canso*, never attained the same recognition as the words and metric scheme. The melodies were (p. 70) "relatively unobtrusive" and were, moreover, always subject to fairly extensive modification by the jongleur performing the song.

[13] D'Arco Silvio Avalle, ed., *Peire Vidal: Poesie*, 2 vols. (Milan: Ricciardi, 1960), 1: 37-43.

[14] Gianluigi Toja, ed., *Arnaut Daniel: Canzoni* (Florence: Sansoni, 1961), p. 271.

[15] The divorce between words and music was probably quite gradual throughout the troubadour tradition. Van der Werf maintains (p. 70) that the *cansos* were "first and foremost poems" and only secondarily musical compositions. By this analysis the increasing independence of the words from the melody was a slow and natural process. The shift from poetry to prose is, however, another matter.

[16] Jean Boutière and Alexander H. Schutz, eds., *Les Biographies des troubadours* (Toulouse and Paris: Privat and Didier, 1950); revised and enlarged by J. Boutière and I. M. Cluzel (Paris: Nizet, 1964), p. 17. All future references to the texts of the *vidas* and *razos* will be indicated in the notes simply by Boutière and Schutz (the 1964 edition being always understood), followed by a page number.

[17] Boutière and Schutz, p. 38.

[18] Boutière and Schutz, p. 216.

[19] Rupert T. Pickens, ed., *The Songs of Jaufré Rudel* (Toronto: Pontifical Institute of Medieval Studies, 1978), pp. 215-41.

[20] Boutière and Schutz, p. 199.

[21] Jeanroy, ed., *Les Chansons de Guillaume IX* (Paris: Champion, 1927), pp. 26-29.

[22] Frank R. Hamlin, Peter T. Ricketts, and John Hathaway, *Introduction à l'étude de l'ancien provençal* (Geneva: Droz, 1967), pp. 141-42.

[23] Lazar, *Bernard*, p. 60.

[24] Zumthor (*Essai de poétique médiévale* [Paris: Seuil, 1972], p. 216) states this coequivalence even more emphatically: "il en résulte qu'un vers comme 'chanson par amors trouvée' doit être considéré comme tautologique." The specific term which I have used, "triangle" or "lyric triangle," was borrowed from Professor Karl D. Uitti, Princeton University.

25 For a discussion of *trobar ric*, see Linda M. Paterson, *Troubadours and Eloquence* (Oxford: Clarendon Press, 1975), pp. 178-85. Dante, of course (*Purgatorio* xxvi, v. 117), pays homage to Arnaut specifically because of his superiority as a craftsman of his mother tongue.

26 Though some scholars would claim that *Las Razos de trobar* is more of a grammarbook than an *ars poetica*, I would argue that it does in fact fulfill its opening promise to teach "la drecha maniera de trobar." See in this regard my article, "The Problem of the Prologue in *Las Razos de trobar*," *Res Publica Litterarum*, forthcoming.

27 Lazar, *Bernard*, pp. 64-66.

28 Robert Scholes (*Structuralism in Literature: An Introduction* [New Haven: Yale University Press, 1974], p. 29), summarizing Roman Jakobson, explains the phenomenon thus: "Jakobson has identified poetry as projecting its language from the metaphoric or paradigmatic axis of verbalization onto the metonymic or syntagmatic. Thus, poetry deliberately opposes the linear, ongoing, diachronic qualities of speech with spatial, obstructive, synchronic qualities." See also Jakobson's own remarks on the poetic function in Roman Jakobson, "Concluding Statement: Linguistics and Poetics," in *Style in Language*, ed. Thomas A. Sebeok (Cambridge, Mass.: M.I.T. Press, 1960), pp. 350-77, esp. p. 358; and Jakobson, "Poetry of Grammar and Grammar of Poetry," *Lingua* 21 (1968): 597-608.

29 For an interesting discussion of binary space (inside vs. outside) in the *canso*, see Jonathan Saville, *The Medieval Erotic Alba: Structure as Meaning* (New York: Columbia University Press, 1972), pp. 228-29.

30 Zumthor (*Essai*, p. 35) points out the use of proverbs and dictums in vernacular lyric poetry as a means of affirming the *auctoritas* of the text.

31 Eliza M. Ghil (*The "Canzo": Structural Study of a Poetic Genre* [Ph.D. dissertation Columbia University, 1978], pp. 194-95) states that the vast majority of *canso* openings (of which the nature beginnings are but one variant) contain "the poet's admission of his own poetic activity in which he is being engaged *hic et nunc*; or—rather—the text's declaration of self-referentiality, of its becoming a text in the listener's/reader's presence." Thus Bernart's *exordium* is perfectly typical of the genre.

32 Stephen G. Nichols, Jr. ("Toward an Aesthetic of the Provençal *Canso*," in *The Disciplines of Criticism*, ed. Peter Demetz, Thomas Greene, and Lowry Nelson, Jr. [New Haven: Yale University Press, 1968], pp. 352-55) stresses the "amazing autonomy" of the individual stanza within a *canso*. There is no linear progression from beginning to end. At the most, stanzas may be paired (*coblas doblas*).

33 For a definition of *tornada*, see Jeanroy, *La Poèsie lyrique des troubadours*, 2: 93-94.

34 Barbara Herrnstein Smith (*Poetic Closure: A Study of how Poems End* [Chicago: University of Chicago Press, 1968], p. 244), though referring specifically to modern poetry, makes the following statement, applicable to the *canso* as well: "Thus, even if a poem is

otherwise well closed in terms of its structure, unwanted finality effects in the concluding lines can be weakened or obscured by . . . allusions to unstable events." Thus the poet can achieve an effect of "terminal suspension."

[35] François J. M. Raynouard, *Lexique roman ou Dictionnaire de la langue des troubadours comparée avec les autres langues de l'Europe latine*, 6 vols. (Heidelberg: Carl Winter, 1836-45), 5: 93-94; Emil Levy, *Provenzalisches Supplement-wörterbuch*, 8 vols. (Leipzig: Reisland, 1894-1924), 7: 343-44; Glynnis M. Cropp, *Le Vocabulaire courtois des troubadours de l'époque classique* (Geneva: Droz, 1975), pp. 93-97.

[36] Boutière and Schutz, pp. 20-21.

[37] Jean-Charles Payen ("*Lo vers es fis e naturaus* [Notes sur la poétique de Bernard de Ventadour]," in *Mélanges d'histoire littéraire de linguistique et de philologie romanes offerts à Charles Rostaing*, 2 vols. [Liège, 1974], 2: 807) examines this verse for what it reveals about "le mécanisme profond de la création poétique" and argues that Bernart sees his creative activity as "une sorte de pulsion biologique ou de nécessité vitale."

[38] One sees in the opening stanza of another song by Bernart de Ventadorn, *Be·m cuidei de chantar sofrir* (Lazar, *Bernard*, p. 108, vv. 3-7) this same notion that the song has the power to bring joy and comfort to those who hear it:

> eras, pus negus no s'esjau
> e pretz e donar vei morir,
> no posc mudar no prenha cura
> d'un vers novel a la frejura,
> que conortz er als autres entre lor.

[39] Allusions to specific people and places occur with surprising frequency. To be assured of this, one need only consult: Frank M. Chambers, *Proper Names in the Lyrics of the Troubadours* (Chapel Hill: University of North Carolina Press, 1971); Wilhelmina M. Wiacek, "Geography in the Provençal Poetry of the Troubadours of the Twelfth and Thirteenth Centuries," in *Mélanges . . . Rostaing*, 2: 1235-43.

[40] For a comment on the pairing of *pretz* and *valor*, see Cropp, pp. 435-38. One finds the juxtaposition of *jauzen* and *pensiu* in *Be m'agrada·l bels tems d'estiu*, in Topsfield, ed., *Les Poésies du troubadour Raimon de Miraval* (Paris: Nizet, 1971), p. 132, v. 20.

[41] Cropp (p. 348) denies that *joi* ever became synonymous with the ultimate experience of love; she believes, rather, that it had a more general sense as "le but de presque toute activité du poète-amoureux." She does admit, however (p. 352): ". . . ressentie dans sa plénitude, la joie représente l'achèvement de la *fin' amor*."

[42] Jauss, 82.

[43] Zumthor (*Essai*, p. 181) remarks that lyric tends to unfold into narrative as soon as an indication of "progressivité" is introduced. The choice of the perfect tense in the verse "je vous ai aimé," for example, implies subsequent cessation of love, followed by memory, hence a narrative progression.

[44] Zumthor (*Essai*, p. 37) stresses this "dramatic" aspect of medieval poetry.

[45] Unlike Mallarmé, the troubadour could not hope for, or even imagine, a private encounter between himself on paper and an individual reader. Even so-called closed poems had to be transmitted by an interpreter, the jongleur, to a group of listeners.

[46] A *senhal* may designate either the patron or the lady to whom the *canso* is dedicated. Jeanroy, *La Poèsie lyrique des troubadours*, 1: 317-20.

[47] For general information about the *vidas* and *razos*, see Boutière and Schutz, Introduction, pp. vii-lviii.

[48] Schutz, "Where were the Provençal *Vidas* and *Razos* Written?", *Modern Philology* 35 (1937-38): 225-32.

[49] Boutière and Schutz, p. viii.

[50] Schutz, "Were the *Vidas* and *Razos* Recited?", *Studies in Philology* 36 (1939): 570.

[51] Schutz ("Prose Style in the Provençal Biographies," *Philological Quarterly* 30 [1951]: 185) recognizes in the *vidas* and *razos* a unique possibility for the comparison of prose and verse syntax of the same period. He further believes that datable mss allow us to trace, in prose, the progress toward a modern conception of prose style. Recent studies, such as the present one and one by Margaret Egan (*The Old Provençal "Vidas": A Textual Analysis* [Ph.D. dissertation Yale University, 1976]), represent preliminary attempts to address such matters.

[52] The shift from first to third person affects the perspective more radically than one might realize. Emile Benveniste (*Problèmes de linguistique générale* [Paris: Gallimard, 1966], pp. 251-57) has revealed that the personal pronouns *je/tu/il* do not constitute a unified class. Whereas *je* and *tu* have no reality out of context, third-person pronouns do. These third-person forms point to a reality beyond the specific instance of discourse where they occur. Thus *il* conveys a different kind of reality from *je/tu*. The shift from the present tense to the past, which goes along with the replacement of *je* by *il*, moves us from the domain of *discours* to the complementary system of speech, called *histoire*.

[53] Benveniste (pp. 237-50) sees the preterite, the tense of *histoire*, as essentially "objective," in that it refers to a time independent of the moment of discourse. Thus, the preterite is the objective tense of the facts themselves, whereas the passé composé, found uniquely in *discours*, is the subjective tense of the person who recounts the facts as a witness or participant.

[54] For a discussion of the various kinds of *je* in medieval narrative, see Zumthor, *Essai*, pp. 172-75.

[55] For further examples of how a named locus may function simultaneously in several different referential schemes, see my article, "The Meeting of Fact and Fiction in an Old Provençal *Razo*," *L'Esprit Créateur* (Winter 1979), 84-94.

Chapter II

[1] Stanislaw Strónski (*La Poèsie et la réalité au temps des troubadours* [Oxford, 1943], p. 22) makes more or less systematic distinctions between those facts of a *vida* which are historically accurate and those which are not. He classifies as true information pertaining to the troubadour's provenance, family, social status, profession, and participation in political developments, and dismisses as unreliable whatever the biographer might have to say about the poet's relationships with women.

[2] The five troubadours for each of whom we possess two relatively independent *vidas* fall into two categories: prolific poets of widespread reputation, whose works were being performed during the late twelfth century when troubadour lyric activity and the enthusiasm for the products of this activity were at their peak (Marcabru, Boutière and Schutz, pp. 10, 12; Bernart de Ventadorn, pp. 20-21, 26-27; and Bertran de Born, pp. 65, 68) and Italian troubadours of comparatively late date (Sordel, pp. 562, 566; Bertolome Zorzi, pp. 576, 579).

[3] Boutière and Schutz, pp. 10, 12.

[4] Boutière and Schutz, pp. 321-28.

[5] Boutière and Schutz, pp. 16-17.

[6] Among the four extant *chansonniers* compiled in the thirteenth century, only *B* puts Guiraut in initial position, but the other mss give him a place of prominence, too. In *A* he is situated second after Peire d'Alvergne, and in *I* and *K* he is located third after Peire d'Alvergne and Peire Rogier.

[7] Boutière and Schutz, pp. 39-40.

[8] D. R. Sutherland ("Flexions and Categories in Old Provençal," *Transactions of the Philological Society* [1959], 45) remarks concerning the use of verb tenses in Old Provençal that the language "shows a marked preference for indicating aspects of the verb such as duration, process, prospect, possibility over purely chronological distinctions." The preterite and the imperfect (compound past, pluperfect, and past anterior) denote degrees of completion in relation to the verbal concept, not degrees of remoteness in time. She points out that there were no fixed rules for the choice of one tense over another and that there was "a great deal of personal freedom in usage" (48).

[9] We read in the *vida* for Peire d'Alvergne (Boutière and Schutz, pp. 263-64): "En Guirautz de Borneill fetz la premeira canson que anc fos faita."

[10] According to Schutz ("Were the *Vidas* and *Razos* Recited?", 570), it was more properly the function of a *razo* than of a *vida* to "furnish a build-up" for coming songs.

[11] According to the classification of Alfred Pillet and Henry Carstens (*Bibliographie der Troubadours* [Halle: Saale, 1933; reprint ed., New York: Burt Franklin, 1968], pp. 202-14), the poems of Guiraut de Borneill span an unusually wide range of genres: *canso, tenso,*

sirventes, sirventes joglaresc, pastorela, romans, planh, alba, devinalh, and crusade song. Moreover, Guiraut has the unique distinction of apparently having converted mid-career from the hermetic *trobar clus* to *trobar leu,* a clear, accessible style which he is responsible for naming and defending as such. See Paterson's discussion of Guiraut's style, pp. 88-144, esp. pp. 139-44.

[12] Boutière and Schutz, p. 59.

[13] For the complete text of *En cest sonet,* see Toja, pp. 271-83.

[14] For a discussion of Arnaut's style, read Paterson, pp. 190-93.

[15] This glorification of the performer within the text of a *vida* corroborates Schutz's geographically based argument that many of the *vidas* were originally composed by jongleurs, who, through their travels, would have gained a precise knowledge of the topography of Southern France. See Schutz, "Where were the Provençal *Vidas* and *Razos* Written?", 231-32.

[16] See my article, "Old Provençal *Vidas* as Literary Commentary," *Romance Philology* 33 (May 1980): 514-15.

[17] See Toja's commentary on this *tornada,* p. 281. He regards these verses as a "spiritual portrait" of the poet who suffers torment as he strives to attain essentially unattainable goals.

[18] In the last full stanza before the *tornada* of *En cest sonet* Arnaut makes it clear that he does not possess the lady whom he loves so much (Toja, p. 274, vv. 36-39):

Ges pel maltraich q'ieu soferi
de ben amar no·m destoli,
si tot me ten en desert,
c'aissi ·n fatz los motz en rima.

[19] Arnaut begins his song thus (Toja, pp. 271-72, vv. 1-4):

En cest sonet coind'e leri
fauc motz e capuig e doli,
que serant verai e cert
qan n'aurai passat la lima.

[20] Boutière and Schutz, pp. 16-17.

[21] The adjective *gentils* is applied to twenty-five troubadours in addition to Jaufré Rudel, but only rarely is it prefaced by an intensifying adverb, e.g. *mout.* Eight troubadours are described as *gentils hom*: Arnaut Daniel (p. 59), Peire de Bussignac (p. 145), Gausbert de Poicibot (p. 229), Peire Rogier (p. 267), Monge de Montaudon (p. 307), Guillem Ademar (p. 349), Lanfranc Cigala (p. 569), and Bertolome Zorzi (p. 576). Eight others are called *gentils castellans*: Gui d'Uisel (p. 202), Rainaut de Pon (p. 219), Garin lo Brun (p. 299), Guillem de Balaun (p. 321), Gauceran de Saint Leidier (p. 338), Garin d'Apchier (p. 343), Bertran del

Pojet (p. 514), and Guillem de Cabestaing (p. 537). Three others are referred to as *gentils bars*: Blacatz (p. 489), Gui de Cavaillo (p. 505), and Guillem de Berguedan (p. 527). Three female troubadours are characterized as *gentils domna*: Na Castelloza (p. 333), Azalais de Porcairagues (p. 341), Na Lombarda (p. 416). Sordel is portrayed as a *gentils catanis* (p. 566). One troubadour besides Jaufré Rudel is depicted as *molt gentils*, Pons de Capdoill, but he is a *molt gentils bars* (p. 311), not a *princes*. The only instance where a troubadour is designated by a *vida* in a manner that would make him more *gentils* than Jaufré Rudel occurs in the *vida* for Blacasset, who is identified as the son of Blacatz "que fon lo meillor gentill hom" (p. 515).

[22] Most recently Pickens (Introduction, p. 1) has stated, I believe, convincingly concerning the historical Jaufré Rudel: "Jaufré was indeed *prince de Blaia*. The lords of Blaye, Pons and Bergerac bore the title *princeps*, a local equivalent of *dominus*."

[23] In Boutière and Schutz, p. 19, n. 3, the editors raise the following question by way of tentative explanation of the phrase *ab paubres motz*: "S'agit-il de la pauvreté effective du vocabulaire de Rudel, ou de la simplicité de son style, contrastant avec le *trobar ric* ou *clus*?" See also my article, "Old Provençal *Vidas* as Literary Commentary," 514.

[24] In MSS. *A* and *B*, however, which like *I* and *K*, date from the thirteenth century, the scribe concludes by announcing that a selection of poems by Jaufré is recorded beneath the *vida* (Boutière and Schutz, p. 17): "E aqui son escriutas de las soas chanssos." For a statistical analysis of the closural patterns in the *vidas*, see nn. 31-33, below.

[25] Pickens, p. 166, vv. 33-35.

[26] Jeanroy (*La Poèsie lyrique des troubadours*, 1:113) has described the process whereby an image from a lyric poem is transferred to the prose of the *vidas* and *razos* as "une métaphore donnant naissance à une anecdote."

[27] To cite only two of the most famous examples: one of the *vidas* for Marcabru (Boutière and Schutz, p. 10) bases itself on the final stanza of *Dirai vos senes duptansa* (J.-M.-L. Dejeanne, ed., *Poèsies complètes du troubadour Marcabru* [Toulouse: Privat, 1909], p. 83, vv. 67-72); one of the *razos* for Bernart de Ventadorn (Boutière and Schutz, p. 29) draws upon the opening verses of *Can vei la lauzeta mover* (Lazar, *Bernard*, p. 180, vv. 1-4).

[28] Boutière and Schutz, pp. 263, 267, 39, 20, 167, 351, 32, 425, 59, 311, 161, 345, 202, 569, 199, 349, 252, 301, 64, 489, 434, 436, 233, 500, 10, 146, 14, 196, 562, 333, 255, 239, 215, 508, 307, 432, 235, 341, 523, 258, 338, 257, 218, 559, 335, 503, 198. I follow here the order of the texts as they occur in MSS. *I* and *K*.

[29] *borc* (Boutière and Schutz, p. 167), *ciutat* (pp. 569, 199), *encontrada* (pp. 59, 341), *evesquat* (pp. 263, 32, 311, 161, 338), *marques* (p. 559). The remaining 36 texts show an unprefaced toponym after *si fo de*.

[30] *joglars* (Boutière and Schutz, pp. 408, 236, 9, 493, 217, 438, 488), *castellans* (p. 65; *rics castellans*, p. 271; *gentils castellans*, pp. 514, 219, 299, 343), *cavalliers* (pp. 149, 530, 513, 495, 147, 420), *gentils hom* (pp. 229, 579; *mout gentils hom*, p. 16), *paubres*

cavalliers (pp. 303, 375, 497), *bars* (*rics baros*, p. 220; *gentils bars*, p. 527), *coms* (p. 284), *clers* (p. 145), *borges* (p. 510), *cantaire* (p. 491), *fills* (pp. 470, 447, 347, 515), *moiller* (p. 445), *major cortes* (p. 7). For an explanation of certain of these terms, see Schutz, "Joglar, borges, cavallier dans les biographies provençales: Essai d'évaluation sémantique," in *Mèlanges de linguistique et de littèrature romanes à la mèmoire d'István Frank* (Sarrebruck, 1957), pp. 672-77.

[31] Boutière and Schutz, pp. 263-64, 408-11, 425-26, 470-71, 311, 447-48, 347, 149-50, 579, 199, 252, 500, 16-17, 255, 215, 236-37, 508, 307-8, 527. An interesting variant of the death of the protagonist as a technique of closure occurs in the well-known *vida* concerning Guillem de Cabestaing (pp. 530-31), where it is the beloved lady, not the poet, whose death (a violent one at that!) brings the account to a close.

[32] religious orders (Boutière and Schutz, pp. 349, 436), abandonment of profession (pp. 202, 64, 239-40), favor at court (pp. 167, 303, 562). In the first category it should be noted that Perdigo (pp. 408-11) entered the order of Cîteaux and then died. Thus, I have counted his *vida* among those which end with death. See n. 31, above.

[33] *vidas* leading into a specific poem (Boutière and Schutz, pp. 267-68, 59, 140-42, 420, 343), *vidas* leading into a corpus of songs (pp. 20-21, 39-40, 311, 229-30, 161-63, 347, 569, 333, 255, 215, 491, 432, 335-36, 147), *vidas* that conclude with a comment on the poet's productivity (pp. 32-33, 345, 301, 515, 513, 514, 196, 341, 445, 257, 495, 219, 559, 299, 503, 488, 145, 198). One might also include in this last category the *vida* for Peire de Valeira (p. 14), which places the key formula denoting poetic activity, *e fez* . . ., in the penultimate sentence and which terminates with a critical remark about the troubadour's songs: "Sei cantar non aguen gran valor, ni el."

[34] Boutière and Schutz, pp. 345, 64, 510, 146, 513, 514, 9, 491, 235, 445, 497, 338, 257, 7, 217, 218, 559, 299, 284, 438, 198. This list can be increased by six if one admits also those texts which contain one present-tense verb in their otherwise preterite account (pp. 59, 489, 10, 196, 432, 503).

Chapter III

[1] Raynouard, 5: 51-52, 6: 36; Levy, 7: 59-65.

[2] *Can la freid' aura venta*, v. 55, in Lazar, *Bernard*, pp. 160-62.

[3] *Ges l'estornels non s'oblida*, vv. 1-2, in Dejeanne, pp. 126-29.

[4] *Era·m cosselhatz, senhor*, vv. 57-60, in Lazar, *Bernard*, pp. 156-58.

⁵*D'un sirventes nom chal far lonhor ganda*, vv. 3-4, in Thomas, pp. 16-18.

⁶*Mon chan fenisc*, vv. 1-4, in Thomas, pp. 24-27.

⁷*Per savi·l tenc ses doptanssa*, vv. 1-4, in Dejeanne, pp. 178-82.

⁸*No sap chantar qui so non di*, vv. 1-4, in Pickens, pp. 215-41.

⁹Boutière and Schutz, p. 75.

¹⁰Thomas, pp. 110-13.

¹¹The classification on the part of the author of the *razo* of this poem as a *sirventes* is all the more interesting when one notes that Pillet and Carstens (p. 72) list it as a *canso*.

¹²*Era·m cosselhatz, senhor*, v. 41, in Lazar, *Bernard*, pp. 156-58.

¹³*Lo tems vai e ven e vire*, vv. 50-52, in Lazar, *Bernard*, pp. 232-34.

¹⁴*Can lo glatz e·l frechs e la neus*, vv. 14-15, in Adolf Kolsen, ed., *Sämtliche Lieder des Trobadors Giraut de Bornelh*, 2 vols. (Halle: Niemeyer, 1910), 1: 58-64.

¹⁵*L'aur' amara*, vv. 69-70, in Toja, pp. 253-69.

¹⁶*En cest sonet coind' e leri*, vv. 19-21, in Toja, pp. 271-83.

¹⁷Cropp, p. 45 and pp. 45-46, n. 90.

¹⁸Cropp would agree with the general argument put forth here, i.e. that in the typical *canso* the troubadour does not analyze the various parts of his lady's body. Indeed she states quite adamantly (p. 161): "Il faut pourtant souligner que les troubadours de l'époque classique décrivent plus rarement qu'on ne l'aurait peut-être attendu les traits physiques de la dame.... Il manque donc un vocabulaire visuel riche et varié, l'observation et le pittoresque font aussi défaut, ce qui montre une fois de plus que les troubadours préfèrent l'abstraction et les qualités morales."

¹⁹For an analysis of how the author of another *razo* mixes fact and fiction within his narrative account, see my article, "The Meeting of Fact and Fiction in an Old Provençal *Razo*."

²⁰Boutière and Schutz, pp. 78-79, 286-87. It should be noted that the *razo* for the Dalfin d'Alvergne is recorded uniquely in MS.*H* and is therefore not among the biographical texts preserved by MSS.*I* and *K*, where the numerous *razos* for Bertran de Born occur.

²¹Sutherland (45) has pointed out the tendency in Old Provençal to use the various past tenses as a means of defining aspect rather than time. See ch. 2, n. 8, above.

²²Boutière and Schutz, pp. 86, 75, 78-79, 81-82, 72-73.

[23] Boutière and Schutz, pp. 361-63.

[24] What I am here calling a linguistically defined space is analogous to Saussure's "circuit de la parole." See Ferdinand de Saussure, *Cours de linguistique gènèrale* (Paris: Payot, 1949), p. 27.

[25] Georges Poulet, *Etudes sur le temps humain: I* (Paris: Editions du Rocher, 1976), pp. 5-11.

[26] Avalle, *Peire Vidal*, 1: 37-43.

[27] For other examples of this expression, see Raynouard, 2: 255.

[28] Avalle, *Peire Vidal*, 1: 47-49.

[29] Avalle, *Peire Vidal*, 2: 322-26.

[30] Avalle, *Peire Vidal*, 2: 367-71.

[31] Boutière and Schutz, pp. 351-52.

[32] See ch. 1, n. 35. Paterson (p. 202) doubts that *trobar ric* ever gained status as a technical term designating a particular style in the same way that *trobar leu* did.

Chapter IV

[1] In addition to *Las Razos de trobar*, Raimon Vidal wrote two long narrative poems, *Abril issia* and *So fo e·l temps*, and possibly a third, the *Castia-gilos*. All references here to *Las Razos de trobar* will come from Marshall's edition, cited above (ch. 1, n. 1). Unless otherwise indicated, I shall be using the *B* version of the text. The *chansonnier* designated *B* by Marshall and others (p. ix) is the same as *P*, which will be described in the next chapter. It is a document of special interest because it contains *vidas, razos*, and *cansos* as well as grammatical texts.

[2] The perfect tense *an saubuda* seems to me especially noteworthy, for it reveals Raimon Vidal's conviction that things were no worse in his day than in former times. Other scholars, however, seem to have overlooked this part of Raimon's remark. Marshall (*The "Razos de trobar*," p. lxxxi) has described *Las Razos* as "Vidal's personal statement-- sometimes having the tone of personal polemic--about what was wrong with poets and poetry in his time." Similarly, A. Ruffinato (*Terramagnino da Pisa: "Doctrina d'Acort"* [Rome, 1968], pp. 33-34) maintains that Raimon Vidal realized with displeasure that the Provençal language was being mistreated in his time by poets, especially Catalan poets who were using it.

[3] The question of whether Raimon framed the prologue to *Las Razos* according to the rules of classical rhetoric is a vexed one. F. Guessard (*Grammaires provençales de Hugues Faidit et de Raymond Vidal de Besaudun* [*XIIIe siècle*], 2nd ed. [Paris, 1858; reprint ed.,

Geneva: Slatkine, 1973], p. xlv), for example, denies that these introductory remarks are based on rhetorical convention: "Cet avertissement... se recommande par une franchise et une liberté de pensée qui ne se cache sous aucune formule de convention." I believe, however, that the opening paragraphs contain all the essential ingredients of a classical prologue and that Raimon Vidal has deliberately incorporated these elements into his work in order to make it as persuasive as possible. For further discussion of this point, see "The Problem of the Prologue."

[4] Martín de Riquer (*História de la literatura catalana*, 4 vols. [Barcelona: Edicions Ariel, 1964], 1: 120) uses this passage as the basis for his claim that Raimon Vidal recognized the existence of traditional or popular poetry that contrasted with the courtly genres. To my mind, however, there is nothing in Raimon's discussion to indicate that he believed that the shepherds were doing anything other than imitating the troubadours.

[5] Concerning the word *galliardias*, consult Guessard (p. xlvi), who translates it by "tous les sentiments vifs et élevés." Interestingly, though Guessard himself is not satisfied with this rendering, subsequent Vidal scholars seem to agree with his interpretation: see Anker Teilgard Laugesen, "*Las Razos de trobar*," in *Etudes romanes dédiées à Andreas Blinkenberg* (Copenhagen: Munksgaard, 1963), 93. Marshall (*The "Razos de trobar*," p. 107, n. 31) translates *galliardias* as "exceptional deeds, bravery." With regard to the word *entendre*, Schutz, in a pair of articles ("Preliminary Study on *Trobar e Entendre*: An Expression in Medieval Aesthetics," *Romanic Review* 23 [1932]: 129-38; and "More on *Trobar e Entendre*," *Romanic Review* 26 [1935]: 29-31), tries to argue that *entendre* has a specific technical meaning having to do with the composition of poetry. Schutz's theory is of particular interest to this essay because a number of the examples which he cites come from *Las Razos de trobar*. Marshall (*The "Razos de trobar*," p. 107, n. 23) disagrees with Schutz and maintains that the ordinary meaning of *entendre* as " 'to comprehend (what others have written)' is acceptable in all contexts in the *Razos* and distinctly preferable in some." I believe that Marshall is correct. The significance of the pair *trobar e entendre* is, as I understand it, that the troubadour is the subject of the first infinitive and that the audience is the subject of the second, and *not* (as Schutz would have it) that the troubadour is the subject of both.

[6] Marshall, *The "Razos de trobar*," p. lxxxii.

[7] *prims* (lines 11, 15, 17, 45, 52, 54, 233, 240, 342, 431, 443, 471), *primamenz* (lines 17, 85, 429), *aprimar* (line 472). In every instance *prim* is used to modify *hom*. The prevalence of this word in Raimon Vidal's text is all the more curious because of its apparently uneven distribution throughout the corpus of troubadour writings. Cropp does not list it in her *Vocabulaire courtois*; Paterson, on the other hand, discusses it rather amply in her *Troubadours and Eloquence* (pp. 136-39). Can we infer from this that *prim* was predominantly a technical term?

[8] Aristide Marigo, ed., *Dante Alighieri: "De Vulgari Eloquentia"* (Florence: Le Monnier, 1957), I, X, 2-4. For discussion of this and other points of comparison between *Las Razos de trobar* and the *De Vulgari Eloquentia*, see ch. 5, below.

[9] Laugesen (90-91) comments briefly on Raimon's terminology: "Raimon a voulu définir *las parladuras de Franza e de Lemozi* comme étant intermédiaires entre la *gramatica* et ce que, suivant l'usage du temps, il appelle le *roman*, c'est à dire l'ensemble des idiomes néo-

latins." Laugesen further remarks that Vidal's *nostres lengages* is apparently analogous to Dante's *nostrum ydioma*.

[10]Marshall (*The "Razos de trobar*," pp. lxxi, lxxx) would deny that any of the material in *Las Razos de trobar* is systematically presented. He sees "the rather unsystematic arrangement of the material" as evidence that the work is above all, "a personal manifesto." With reference to this central section, Marshall faults Vidal for beginning with a threefold classification of words, which then plays no further part in the grammatical exposition. But Marshall reserves his harshest judgment for Vidal's ending: "The final paragraphs of the work (lines 435-68) give the impression of being stray jottings on a variety of subjects."

[11]"Las autras paraulas del verb, per so car ieu no las poiria dir sens gran affan, totz hom prims las deu ben esgardar et usar cant au parlar las gentz d'aqella terra . . ." (lines 430-32).

[12]lines 232-34.

[13]"Per aqi mezeis deu gardar, si vol far un cantar o un romans, qe diga rasons et paraulas continuadas et proprias et avinenz, et qe sos cantars o sos romans non sion de paraulas biaisas ni de doas parladuras ni de razons mal continuadas ni mal seguidas" (lines 451-54).

[14]Lazar, *Bernard*, pp. 92-94.

[15]*Iausen-pensiu* comes from a *canso* by Raimon de Miraval, *Be m'agrada·l bels tems d'estiu* (Topsfield, p. 132, v. 20). See ch. 1, n. 40, above. *Mos mals aitan bos* occurs in Bernart de Ventadorn's *Non es meravelha s'eu chan* (Lazar, *Bernard*, p. 60, v. 31). Another striking example of such oxymoron is found in Bernart's *canso Can lo boschatges es floritz* (Lazar, *Bernard*, p. 224, v. 9), in which he declares: "Per midons m'esjau no-jauzitz."

[16]Marshall, *The "Razos de trobar*," p. lxxix. Likewise, Salvatore Santangelo (*Dante e i trovatori provenzali* [Catania: Giannotta, 1921], pp. 94-95) claims that anyone who examines the introduction of the *Razos de trobar* will surely be struck by the contrast between the promises made in the opening paragraphs and the treatise as a whole.

[17]Marigo, p. xxxi.

[18]reis sui d'Aragon, ieu sui rics homs, line 112; verges es aqest homs, verges es aqesta femna, line 131; bon m'es car m'aves onrat, line 144; bo·m sap l'escut, line 164; vengut son los cavaliers, line 167; ieu mi fas gai, ieu mi teng per pagat, line 246; mal me fai l'anars, bo·m sap le venirs, lines 254-55; ieu feric un home, line 424.

[19]lines 72-75.

[20]"Et tot l'ome qe en aqellas terras son nat ni norit an la parladura natural et drecha. Mas cant uns d'els es eiciz de la parladura per una rima qe i aura mestier o per autra causa, miels o conois cels qe a la parladura reconeguda" (lines 64-67). ". . . et deu ben gardar qe neguna rima qe li aia mestier non la metta fora de sa proprietat ni de son cas ni de son genre ni de son nombre ni de sa part ni de son mot ni de son temps ni de sa persona ni de son alongamen ni de son abreuiamen" (lines 446-50).

[21] The texts of both of these grammatical works may be found in Marshall, *The "Razos de trobar,"* pp. 29-53, 56-91.

[22] Marshall, *The "Razos de trobar,"* pp. lxxi-lxxii, lxxxvi-lxxxix.

[23] Marshall, *The "Razos de trobar,"* pp. lxxii-lxxv, lxxxix-xciii.

[24] See James J. Murphy, *Rhetoric in the Middle Ages: A History of Rhetorical Theory from Saint Augustine to the Renaissance* (Berkeley: University of California Press, 1974), p. 32.

[25] Marshall, ed., *The "Donatz Proensals" of Uc Faidit* (London: Oxford University Press, 1969), pp. 66-78.

[26] The *Leys d'Amors* was the code established by seven troubadours under the directorship of Guilhem Molinier who had organized themselves at Toulouse in 1323 for the purpose of maintaining the cult of poetry through the holding of an annual poetic contest. The *Leys* was tremendously influential, especially in Catalonia; it kept Old Provençal alive as a language of poetry for well over a century. Moreover, in recent times it has provided philologists with precious information about the language of the troubadours. The text may be found in Joseph Anglade, ed., *Las Leys d'Amors,* 4 vols. (Toulouse: Privat, 1919-20).

[27] R. H. Robins, *Ancient and Mediaeval Grammatical Theory in Europe* (London: Bell, 1951), pp. 75-77.

[28] Murphy, pp. 144-46.

Chapter V

[1] For a brief description of each of these mss, see Boutière and Schutz, pp. xv-xix. *ABIK* date from the 13th century, *EPR* from the 14th. *ABIK* present more biographical texts than the later *EPR* group. In *ABIK* each biography precedes a poem or poems. In *EPR* the biographies stand together, apart from the anthology of poems. The 14th-century *chansonniers* show a much higher proportion of *razos* to *vidas* than the earlier mss.

[2] *F*, a 14th-century ms, though containing no *vidas*, presents the same *razos* in the same order as *IK*. But whereas in *F razos* precede their poems, in *IK* they immediately follow their poems. See Boutière and Schutz, pp. xix, 70.

[3] Avalle, *La Letteratura medievale in lingua d'oc nella sua tradizione manoscritta* (Turin: Giulio Einaudi, 1961), pp. 92-93.

[4] Boutière and Schutz, pp. 7, 236-37.

[5] Boutière and Schutz, pp. 569, 220.

[6] Boutière and Schutz, pp. 16-17, 559.

[7] Boutière and Schutz, pp. 514, 235.

[8] Boutière and Schutz, p. xviii, n. 30.

[9] Boutière and Schutz, pp. 72-137.

[10] *A*, now in Rome at the Vatican Library, is the product of an Italian hand. It contains, with its songs, miniatures and 52 *vidas*. *B*, now in Paris at the Bibliothèque Nationale, was written in Provence in the 13th century. It contains songs and 37 *vidas*. See Boutière and Schutz, p. xvi.

[11] No one to my knowledge has looked for thematic unity in the biographies of *I*. Guido Favati (*Biografie di trovatori* [*Testi provenzali dei secoli XIII e XIV*] [Geneva: Bozzi, 1970], pp. 24-25, 25-26, 28) has found a dominant theme in each of the major *chansonniers* where biographical texts are grouped together and stand independent of poems. In *E*, for instance, the scribe shows a preference for love stories with unhappy endings. The compiler of *R* likes tales built around a joke of some sort. The copyist of *P*, in Favati's view, has a special fondness for the theme of a lost love regained.

[12] Boutière and Schutz, pp. 220, 284, 335-36, 470-71, 375-76.

[13] Marshall, *The "Razos de trobar,"* pp. ix-x. See also ch. 4, n. 1, above.

[14] Favati, p. 28. Thomas Bergin (*Dante* [New York: Orion Press, 1965], p. 81) disagrees: "The *razos* of the *chansonniers* are without plan or purpose."

[15] Boutière and Schutz, pp. 187-88, 465-66, 153-55, 314-15, 244-45, 544-49.

[16] Boutière and Schutz, pp. 229-30, 307-8. Though the main part of the Monge de Montaudon's *vida* takes place outside the monastery, the focus shifts to a priory in Spain where the troubadour finished out his days.

[17] Boutière and Schutz, pp. 392-95, 205-6, 425-26.

[18] Marshall, *The "Razos de trobar,"* pp. ix-xiii. In *H* (end of 14th century) and *L* (end of 13th century) *Las Razos de trobar* is set in a context consisting solely of treatises on grammar and poetics. In *C* (late 16th century) it is accompanied by the *Donatz proensals* and some *vidas*. In *R* (mid-14th century) it is placed with other treatises and an anthology of 19 Catalan poems. *B* (early 14th century), also known as *P*, was the subject of our brief discussion.

[19] Marshall, *The "Razos de trobar,"* p. x. The two Old French texts appended to *P* are: *Le Blasme des femmes* and the *Livre des Moralitez*.

[20] Fredi Chiappelli, ed., *Dante Alighieri: Vita Nuova - Rime* (Milan: Mursia, 1965). Bergin (p. 67) has said of the *Vita Nuova*: "It is certainly one of the earliest examples since the classics of a coherent and carefully planned 'book' in the modern sense of the word." He

nonetheless admits (p. 81): "Dante may well have found the usage of the chansonniers appropriate to his purpose."

[21] Charles S. Singleton, *An Essay on the "Vita Nuova"* (Cambridge, Mass.: Harvard University Press, 1949), pp. 25-54.

[22] Much of what is said here about the arrangement of poems in the *Vita Nuova* comes from the introductory remarks of Mark Musa, trans., *Dante: La Vita Nuova* (Bloomington: Indiana University Press, 1962), pp. VII-VIII.

[23] Musa, p. XIII; J. E. Shaw, *Essays on the "Vita Nuova"* (Princeton and Paris: Princeton University Press and Presses Universitaires de France, 1929), pp. 77-108, esp. pp. 90-91.

[24] *Vita Nuova XI, XXIX, XXVIII*. Singleton (p. 34) comments thus on these two digressions: "In order to write . . . in this way, this scribe has had to become what he himself had supplied a name for in concluding his reasons for not writing of Beatrice's death. That, he says, he will leave to some other *chiosatore* 'glossator.' " Further into his essay Singleton (p. 53) describes the whole of the *Vita Nuova* as "a text of poems with a gloss and then yet another gloss."

[25] Passages in which Dante refers to the narrative sections as *ragioni*: XXXV "E però che per questa ragione è assai manifesto, si nollo dividerò" (Chiappelli, p. 69); XXXVI "Ed è piano sanza dividerlo, per la sua precedente ragione" (Chiappelli, p. 70); XXXVII "Potrebbe bene ancora ricevere più divisioni, ma sariano indarno, però che è manifesto per la precedente ragione" (Chiappelli, p. 71); XXXIX "Questo sonetto non divido però che assai lo manifesta la sua ragione" (Chiappelli, p. 73); XL "Questo sonetto non divido, però che assai lo manifesta la sua ragione" (Chiappelli, p. 74).

[26] Singleton, pp. 51-52; G. Folena, "Dante et les troubadours," in *Actes et mémoires du IIIe Congrès international de langue et littérature du Midi de la France, Bordeaux 1961* (Bordeaux, 1965), 25; Vincenzo Crescini, "Le *Razos* provenzali e le prose della V.N.," *Giornale storico della letteratura italiana* 32 (1898): 463-64. Karl Vossler (*Medieval Culture: An Introduction to Dante and his Times*, trans. William Cranston Lawton. 2 vols. [New York: Harcourt, Brace, 1929], 2: 54) argues that at best the *razos* would have furnished "only an additional fortuitous and uncertain suggestion for the artistic form of the *Vita Nuova*."

[27] Chiappelli, pp. 37, 44.

[28] Chiappelli, p. 63.

[29] All citations from the *De Vulgari Eloquentia* will be based on the Marigo edition, cited above. See ch. 4, n. 8. On the matter of whether Dante knew *Las Razos de trobar* when he wrote the *De Vulgari Eloquentia*, most scholars agree that he did. For example, A. Ewert ("Dante's Theory of Language," *The Modern Language Review* 35 [1940]: 357) states: "It is improbable—one might say impossible—that Dante should have remained in ignorance of

Raimon Vidal's work." Santangelo (p. 115), while denying that Dante had any acquaintance with any of the *vidas* and *razos* nevertheless believes that Dante knew *Las Razos de trobar*, not as it has survived but in some longer form.

[30] *Las Razos de trobar*, lines 62-64; *De Vulgari Eloquentia*, I, VIII, 7-9.

[31] *Las Razos de trobar*, lines 77-83; *De Vulgari Eloquentia*, I, VIII, 6. Roger Dragonetti (*Aux Frontières du langage poètique* [*Etudes sur Dante, Mallarmè, Valèry*] [Ghent: Romanica Gandensia, 1961], p. 27) remarks that all of these shared words are, metaphysically speaking, fundamental, that is they pertain to existence and the nature of the world.

[32] *Las Razos de trobar*, lines 59-64; *De Vulgari Eloquentia*, I, VIII, 6. For Dante the fact that the Romance languages have so many words in common is the proof of their common origin.

[33] *De Vulgari Eloquentia*, I, IX, 6-10. Language changes over time and varies from one place to another because of the essential inconstancy of the human race.

[34] *Las Razos de trobar*, lines 85, 90, and lines 138, 146, 147. *De Vulgari Eloquentia*, I, I, 3: "Est et inde alia locutio secundaria nobis, quam Romani gramaticam vocaverunt. Hanc quidem secundariam Greci habent et alii, sed non omnes; ad habitum vero huius pauci perveniunt, quia non nisi per spatium temporis et studii assiduitatem regulamur et doctrinamur in illa." See also *De Vulgari Eloquentia*, I, IX, 11, where Dante defines gramatica thus: "Gramatica nichil aliud est quam quedam inalterabilis locutionis idemptitas diversis temporibus atque locis."

[35] *De Vulgari Eloquentia*, I, VII.

[36] *De Vulgari Eloquentia*, II, I, 1: II, III.

[37] *De Vulgari Eloquentia*, I, XI-XV. Ewert (pp. 359-60) comments: "When we come to the description of the linguistic condition of Italy, the search for the *vulgare illustre*, and the remarks on its use for literary purposes, we have to do with a series of original observations and deductions which reveal Dante as a philologist entitled to a fuller tribute than he has yet received."

[38] *De Vulgari Eloquentia*, I, XVI, 1.

[39] Marshall, *The "Razos de trobar*," p. 108, n. 62-64. The association between the *Lemosi* dialect and literary usage was natural enough, since a surprising number of the most famous troubadours came from this region. The biographers explicitly identify the following poets as being from *Lemosi*: Bernart de Ventadorn (Boutière and Schutz, p. 20), Guiraut de Borneill (p. 39), Bertran de Born (in the *ER* version only, p. 68), Gaucelm Faidit (p. 167), Gui d'Uisel (p. 202), Maria de Ventadorn (p. 212), Uc de la Bacalaria (p. 218), and Gausbert de Poicibot (p. 229).

[40] *Las Razos de trobar*, lines 72-75. See ch. 4, n. 8.

[41] *De Vulgari Eloquentia*, I, X, 2-4. While certain scholars, e.g. Dragonetti (pp. 9-10), continue to say that Dante's purpose in writing the *De Vulgari Eloquentia* was to defend the vulgar language and show that it surpassed Latin in nobility, Ewert (p. 357) has defined Dante's purpose thus: "In fact, the *De Vulgari Eloquentia* is to my mind to be described not as a vindication of the vulgar tongue against Latin, but rather as a challenge issued on behalf of the Italian vernacular against the rather exclusive claims made for Provençal by such writers as Raimon Vidal."

LIST OF WORKS CITED

Anglade, Joseph, ed. *Las Leys d'Amors*. 4 vols. Toulouse: Privat, 1919-20.

Avalle, D'Arco Silvio. *La Letteratura medievale in lingua d'oc nella sua tradizione manoscritta*. Turin: Giulio Einaudi, 1961.

Avalle, D'Arco Silvio, ed. *Peire Vidal: Poesie*. 2 vols. Milan: Ricciardi, 1960.

Benveniste, Emile. *Problèmes de linguistique générale*. Paris: Gallimard, 1966.

Bergin, Thomas. *Dante*. New York: Orion Press, 1965.

Boutière, Jean and Schutz, Alexander H., eds. *Les Biographies des troubadours*. 2nd ed., revised and expanded. Edited by Boutière and I. M. Cluzel. Paris: Nizet, 1964.

Chambers, Frank M. *Proper names in the Lyrics of the Troubadours*. Chapel Hill: University of North Carolina Press, 1971.

Chiappelli, Fredi, ed. *Dante Alighieri: Vita Nuova-Rime*. Milan: Mursia, 1965.

Crescini, Vincenzo. "Le *Razos* provenzali e le prose della *Vita Nuova*." *Giornale storico della letteratura italiana* 32 (1898): 463-64.

Cropp, Glynnis M. *Le Vocabulaire courtois des troubadours de l'époque classique*. Geneva: Droz, 1975.

Dejeanne, J.-M.-L., ed. *Poèsies complètes du troubadour Marcabru*. Toulouse: Privat, 1909.

Dragonetti, Roger. *Aux Frontières du langage poétique (Etudes sur Dante, Mallarmé, Valéry)*. Ghent: Romanica Gandensia, 1961.

Egan, Margaret. "The Old Provençal *Vidas*: A Textual Analysis." Ph.D. dissertation. Yale University, 1976.

Ewert, A. "Dante's Theory of Language." *Modern Language Review* 35 (1940): 355-66.

Favati, Guido. *Biografie di trovatari (Testi provenzali dei secoli XIII e XIV)*. Geneva: Bozzi, 1970.

Folena, G. "Dante et les troubadours." In *Actes et mémoires du IIIe Congrès international de langue et littérature du Midi de la France, Bordeaux 1961*, pp. 21-34. Bordeaux, 1965.

Ghil, Eliza M. "The 'Canzo': Structural Study of a Poetic Genre." Ph.D. dissertation, Columbia University, 1978.

Guessard, F. *Grammaires provençales de Hugues Faidit et de Raymond Vidal de Besaudun* (*XIIIe siècle*). 2nd ed. Paris, 1858; reprint ed., Geneva: Slatkine, 1973.

Hamlin, Frank R.; Ricketts, Peter T.; and Hathaway, John, eds. *Introduction à l'étude de l'ancien provençal*. Geneva: Droz, 1967.

Jakobson, Roman. "Poetry of Grammar and Grammar of Poetry." *Lingua* 21 (1968): 597-608.

Jakobson, Roman. "Concluding Statement: Linguistics and Poetics." in *Style in Language*, pp. 350-77. Edited by Thomas A. Sebeok. Cambridge, Mass.: M.I.T. Press, 1960.

Jauss, Hans-Robert. "Littérature médiévale et théorie des genres." *Poétique* 1 (1970): 79-98.

Jeanroy, Alfred. *La Poésie lyrique des troubadours*. 2 vols. Toulouse and Paris: Privat and Didier, 1934.

Kolsen, Adolf, ed. *Sämtliche Lieder des Trobadors Giraut de Bornelh*. 2 vols. Halle: Niemeyer, 1910.

Laugesen, Anker Teilgård. "*Las Razos de trobar*." In *Etudes romanes dédiées à Andreas Blinkenberg*, pp. 84-96. Copenhagen: Munksgaard, 1963.

Lazar, Moshé. *Amour courtois et fin'amors dans la littérature du XIIe siècle*. Paris: Klincksieck, 1964.

Lazar, Moshé, ed. *Bernard de Ventadour, troubadour du XIIe siècle: Chansons d'amour*. Paris: Klincksieck, 1966.

Levy, Emil. *Provenzalisches Supplementwörterbuch*. 8 vols. Leipzig: Reisland, 1894-1924.

Linskill, Joseph, ed. *The Poems of the Troubadour Raimbaut de Vaqueiras*. The Hague: Mouton, 1964.

Marigo, Aristide, ed. *Dante Alighieri: "De Vulgari Eloquentia."* Florence: Le Monnier, 1957.

Marshall, J. H., ed. *The "Donatz Proensals" of Uc Faidit*. London: Oxford University Press, 1969.

Marshall, J. H. "The Isostrophic *descort* in the Poetry of the Troubadours." *Romance Philology* 35 (1981): 130-57.

Marshall, J. H., ed. *The "Razos de Trobar" of Raimon Vidal and Associated Texts*. London: Oxford University Press, 1972.

Marshall, J. H. "Le Vers au XIIe siècle: genre poétique?" In *Actes et mémoires du IIIe Congrès international de langue et littérature du Midi de la France, Bordeaux 1961*. Bordeaux, 1965, pp. 55-63.

Murphy, James J. *Rhetoric in the Middle Ages: A History of Rhetorical Theory from Saint Augustine to the Renaissance.* Berkeley: University of California Press, 1974.

Musa, Mark, trans. *Dante: La Vita Nuova.* Bloomington: Indiana University Press, 1962.

Nichols, Stephen G., Jr. "Toward an Aesthetic of the Provençal *Canso.*" In *The Disciplines of Criticism*, pp. 349-74. Edited by Peter Demetz, Thomas Greene, and Lowry Nelson, Jr. New Haven: Yale University Press, 1968.

Paterson, Linda M. *Troubadours and Eloquence.* Oxford: Clarendon Press, 1975.

Pattison, Walter T., ed. *The Life and Works of the Troubadour Raimbaut d'Orange.* Minneapolis: University of Minnesota Press, 1952.

Payen, Jean-Charles. "Lo vers es fis e naturaus (Notes sur la poétique de Bernard de Ventadour)." In *Mélanges d'histoire littéraire, de linguistique et de philologie romanes offerts à Charles Rostaing.* 2 vols. Liège, 1974. Vol. 2, pp. 807-17.

Pickens, Rupert T., ed. *The Songs of Jaufré Rudel.* Toronto: Pontifical Institute of Medieval Studies, 1978.

Pillet, Alfred and Carstens, Henry. *Bibliographie der Troubadours.* Halle: Saale, 1933; reprint ed., New York: Burt Franklin, 1968.

[Poe], Elizabeth Wilson. "The Meeting of Fact and Fiction in an Old Provençal *Razo.*" *L'Esprit Créateur* (Winter 1979): 84-94.

[Poe], Elizabeth Wilson. "Old Provençal *Vidas* as Literary Commentary." *Romance Philology* 33 (1980): 510-18.

Poe, Elizabeth Wilson. "The Problem of the Prologue in *Las Razos de Trobar.*" *Res Publica Litterarum*, forthcoming.

Poulet, Georges. *Etudes sur le temps humain: I.* Paris: Editions du Rocher, 1976.

Raynouard, François J. M. *Lexique roman ou Dictionnaire de la langue des troubadours comparée avec les autres langues de l'Europe latine.* 6 vols. Heidelberg: Carl Winter, 1836-45.

de Riquer, Martin. *Història de la literatura catalana.* 4 vols. Barcelona: Edicions Ariel, 1964.

Robins, R. H. *Ancient and Mediaeval Grammatical Theory in Europe.* London: Bell, 1951.

Ruffinato, A. *Terramagnino da Pisa: "Doctrina d'Acort."* Rome: Edizioni dell'Ateneo, 1968.

Santangelo, Salvatore. *Dante e i trovatori provenzali.* Catania: Giannotta, 1921.

de Saussure, Ferdinand. *Cours de linguistique générale*. Paris: Payot, 1949.

Saville, Jonathan. *The Medieval Erotic Alba: Structure as Meaning*. New York: Columbia University Press, 1972.

Scholes, Robert. *Structuralism in Literature: An Introduction*. New Haven: Yale University Press, 1974.

Schutz, Alexander H. "Joglar, borges, cavallier dans les biographies provençales: Essai d'évaluation sémantique." In *Mélanges de linguistique et de littérature romanes à la mémoire d'István Frank*, pp. 672-77, Saarbrücken, 1957.

Schutz, Alexander H. "More on *Trobar e Entendre*." *Romanic Review* 26 (1935): 29-31.

Schutz, Alexander H. "Preliminary Study on *Trobar e Entendre:* An Expression in Medieval Aesthetics." *Romanic Review* 23 (1932): 129-38.

Schutz, Alexander H. "Prose Style in the Provençal Biographies." *Philological Quarterly* 30 (1951): 179-85.

Schutz, Alexander H. "Were the *Vidas* and *Razos* Recited?" *Studies in Philology* 36 (1939): 565-70.

Schutz, Alexander H. "Where were the Provençal *Vidas* and *Razos* Written?" *Modern Philology* 35 (1937-38): 225-32.

Singleton, Charles S. *An Essay on the "Vita Nuova."* Cambridge, Mass.: Harvard University Press, 1949.

Smith, Barbara Herrnstein. *Poetic Closure: A Study of How Poems End*. Chicago: University of Chicago Press, 1968.

Stróński, Stanislaw. *La Poésie et la réalité au temps des troubadours*. Oxford, 1943.

Sutherland, D. R. "Flexions and Categories in Old Provençal." *Transactions of the Philological Society* (1950): 25-70.

Thiolier-Mejean, Suzanne. *Les Poèsies satiriques et morales des troubadours du XIIe siècle à la fin du XIIIe siècle*. Paris: Nizet, 1978.

Thomas, Antoine, ed. *Poésies complètes de Bertran de Born*. Toulouse: Privat, 1888.

Toja, Gianluigi, ed. *Arnaut Daniel: Canzoni*. Florence: Sansoni, 1961.

Topsfield, L. T., ed. *Les Poèsies du troubadour Raimon de Miraval*. Paris: Nizet, 1971.

Topsfield, L. T. *Troubadours and Love*. Cambridge: Cambridge University Press, 1975.

Vossler, Karl. *Medieval Culture: An Introduction to Dante and his Times.* 2 vols. New York: Harcourt, Brace, 1929.

van der Werf, Hendrik. *The Chansons of the Troubadours and Trouvères: A Study of the Melodies and their Relation to the Poems.* Utrecht: A. Oosthoek's Uitgeversmaatschappij NV, 1972.

Wiacek, Wilhelmina M. "Geography in the Provençal Poetry of the Troubadours of the Twelfth and Thirteenth Centuries." In *Mélanges d'histoire littéraire, de linguistique et de philologie romanes offerts à Charles Rostaing.* 2 vols. Liège, 1974. Vol. 2, pp. 1235-43.

Zumthor, Paul. "Classes and Genres in Medieval Literature," pp. 27-36. In *A Medieval Miscellany: Papers of the 1970 Kansas Conference on Medieval Literature.* Edited by Norris J. Lacy. Lawrence: University of Kansas Press, 1972.

Zumthor, Paul. *Essai de poétique médiévale.* Paris: Seuil, 1972.